THE DISNEY

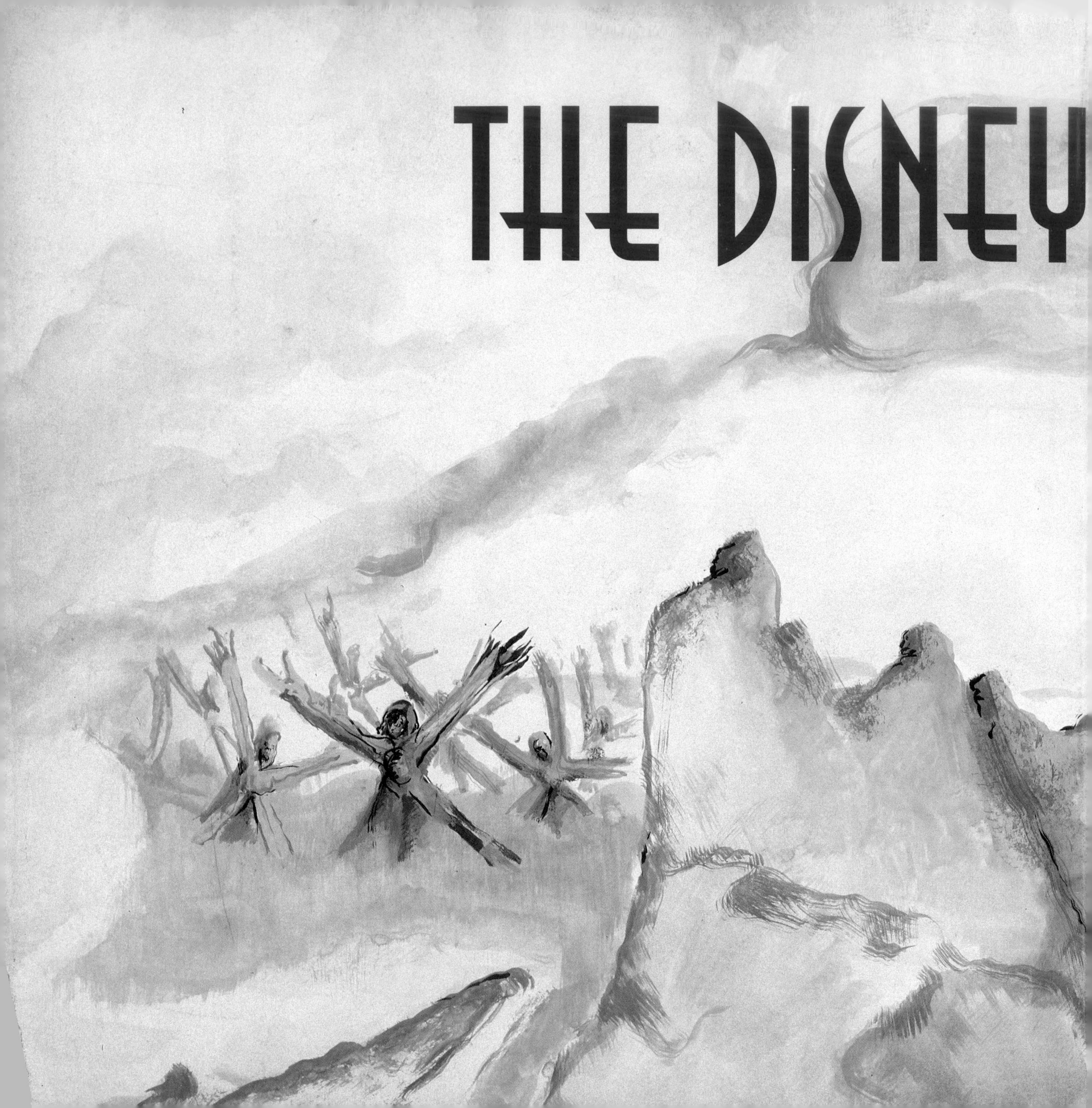

THAT NEVER WAS

The Stories and Art from Five Decades of Unproduced Animation

CHARLES SOLOMON

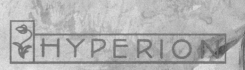HYPERION

For S., *ab marte cum gratia*

Songs from "Hansel and Gretel"
Words and Music by Richard B. Sherman
© 1968 Wonderland Music Company, Inc.
All rights reserved. Used by permission.

Library of Congress Cataloging-in-Publication Data
Solomon, Charles.
The Disney that never was / Charles Solomon.—1st ed.
p.   cm.
Includes bibliographical references and index.
ISBN 0-7868-6037-5
1. Walt Disney Company. 2. Unfinished animated films—United States—
History. I. Title.
NC1766.U52D564 1995
741.5'8'0979493—dc20
95–3053
CIP
FIRST EDITION

10 9 8 7 6 5 4 3 2 1

Page i
"Chanticleer."
Artist: Marc Davis;
medium: watercolor, pen and ink.

Pages ii-iii
"Don Quixote."
Artist: unknown;
medium: watercolor.

CONTENTS

"The Emperor's Nightingale."
Artist: unknown; medium: watercolor, charcoal.

A drawing for the short *Navy Mickey* displays the charm and vitality that won the hearts of millions of fans during the 1930's, including Franklin Delano Roosevelt, Mary Pickford, King George V of England, and the Nizam of Hyderabad. Artist: unknown; medium: charcoal, pencil, colored pencil.

ACKNOWLEDGMENTS

*I love the nostalgic myself. I hope we
never lose some of the things of the past.*
—Walt Disney

MY LAST BOOK, *Enchanted Drawings*, represented nearly a decade and a half of research. When it was completed, I wondered if I had anything left to say about animation. My good friend arts writer Lewis Segal convinced me that my next book should be "a more detailed study, rather than another general history—something vertical, rather than horizontal." Then Disney artist/voice actor Tony Anselmo showed me artwork from some of the uncompleted films in the Disney Animation Research Library. The drawings were simply too beautiful to leave in their folders; they deserved to be seen by a wider audience. So I went to work on another, more vertical animation book.

The bulk of my research was conducted at the Animation Research Library; Manager Kay Salz went out of her way to make working there an enjoyable experience. My thanks to her and her helpful staff—Laurence Ishino, Susie Lee, Adina Lerner, Ariel Levin, and especially, Doug Engalla—who dug out countless folders of artwork, searched for missing or misfiled items, and photocopied numerous pages of notes with unflagging good cheer. Dave Smith and the staff of the Disney Archives provided additional information and answers. Most of my inquiries were fielded by Robert Tieman ("that *is* an interesting question"), who was always ready to track down a needed fact.

At the Walt Disney Studio: Jeffrey Katzenberg, Roy E. Disney, Peter Schneider, Tom Schumaker, Don Hahn, Howard Green (who's put up with sixteen years of my questions and complaints), and his capable assistant, Fumi Kitahara, assisted my efforts in various ways. Many of the artists at Disney Feature Animation offered encouragement, support, and knowledge: Andreas Deja, Raoul Garcia, Eric Goldberg, Glen Keane, Duncan Marjoribanks, Nik Ranieri, and Tom Sito. Four of Disney's justly celebrated "nine old men," Marc Davis, Ollie Johnston, Ward Kimball, and Frank Thomas, and several other artists—Ken Anderson, Vance Gerry, Joe Grant, Bob Kurtz, Burny Mattinson, Bill Peet, Leo Salkin, Tyrus Wong—generously gave their time in interviews and answered additional questions.

Animation scholar John Canemaker graciously shared his research into the making of both the completed and unmade sections of *Fantasia*.

Alex Rannie provided information about music for the Disney films, especially *Fantasia*. Dennis M. Johnson once again lent his skills as a proofreader, catching his usual quota of typos.

Despite my best efforts, I've yet to exhaust the patience of my agent, Bob Cornfield. This book began with Martha Kaplan as its editor; when she gave up editing, it passed to Vicki di Stasio. Rick Kot (a.k.a. Third Editor) inherited it, and prepared the final text with care and discernment. When Kay Salz left the ARL, Lella Smith took over, providing additional encouragement and friendship. Michelle Kilbourne of Walt Disney Imagineering shot all of the artwork. Designer Dana Levy's enthusiasm for the material and discerning graphic sense made working with him an additional pleasure.

Writers love to complain, and several good friends supplied counsel and reasonably sympathetic ears when I fussed about how this book was driving me crazy: Bruce Bardfield, Paul Basta, Kevin Caffey, Greg Clarke, Joe Cocozza, Pat Connolly-Sito, Susan Goldberg, Deitrik Hohenegger, Scott Johnston, Martha Kaplan, Lee Nordling, Jim Panos, Anne Pautler, Jim Brunet, and Stuart Sumida.

My family—Rose Solomon, Ann M. Solomon, Socrates the Arnab, Marsha and Marvin Francis—continued to encourage what others might consider an aberrant interest in animation.

Charles Solomon
February 1995

This anonymous caricature of Walt Disney as Don Quixote was discovered among the preliminary sketches for the film. The artists frequently referred to Disney's expressive eyebrows. Medium: charcoal, pastels.

INTRODUCTION

AS THE DISCOVERY of an unfinished obelisk in an ancient quarry revealed how the Egyptians carved Cleopatra's Needle from a gargantuan block of granite, an examination of some of the hundreds of films the studio artists began to develop but didn't complete offers special insights into the creation of the classic Disney shorts and features.

Unlike their counterparts at other animation studios, the Disney artists saved much of their work—storyboard drawings, preliminary sketches, inspirational studies, animation drawings, backgrounds, and memos from both completed and uncompleted films. Secretaries took notes at story meetings, which were transcribed (sometimes by students in local typing schools) and kept in files with the artwork.

Walt Disney frequently moved individual projects in and out of production as the studio's finances and the progress of competing ideas dictated. Preproduction work began on *Peter Pan* during the early forties and continued off and on until the film was completed in 1953. Keeping previously developed material on hand enabled the artists to pick up where they left off.

Although decades would pass before this

material was accorded the status of fine art and/or collectible, Disney must have realized that it constituted an extraordinary resource for his artists. More than fifty years after the films were made, an animator who wants to study a scene from *Snow White* or *Brave Little Tailor* can flip the original animation drawings and read Disney's comments. When production began on *Pocahontas,* the artists examined preliminary sketches and research from other projects involving Native Americans, including *Hiawatha.*

Some of the films were abandoned for obvious reasons—a lack of time, money, or enough trained artists and the pressures of producing entertainment features and military training films during World War II. Some stories proved too weak to sustain an eighty-minute feature or a seven-minute short. Others were too long or complex, or centered on characters and actions that weren't suited to animation. The reasons for abandoning some seemingly promising ideas have been forgotten.

Drawings and notes survive from hundreds of uncompleted shorts and features. After languishing for decades in pasteboard portfolios, these papers have recently been transferred to the protection of acid-free archival boxes. The material reveals the inner workings of the Disney studio: Nearly thirty years after his death, researchers can see Walt Disney at work, both the visionary who imagined *Snow White and the Seven Dwarfs* and the man who faced the daily problems of running a studio. A discussion held on November 2, 1939, with director Frank Tashlin about the proposed Donald Duck short "Museum Keepers" illustrates Disney's concerns. Tashlin wanted to add scenes depicting a crowd of critics and museumgoers; Disney objected for artistic and practical reasons:

WALT: Those foreign characters coming in this complicates our animation problems. The fellows are used to drawing the Duck and we can get a certain personality into the Duck that will stand up, but when we get into some of those other characters it can look very tacky, you know.

FRANK: But look at *Ferdinand,* Walt. There's a whole slew of characters. . . .

WALT: You don't get the idea. I don't have the men. We have to keep them in the features. We're committed over there. We have to keep those things going. We have men over here [in the shorts division] that are coming along that can learn the game through characters they know. On *Ferdinand,* I took all the men from *Snow White.* We can make it if we stick to those characters that we know, characters that we have good models for.

Although Disney kept more thorough records than any other animation studio, not everything was saved, especially on the uncompleted films. Some folders contain hundreds of detailed drawings and notes that trace the development of an idea over months or even years; others hold a handful of unsigned rough sketches. A few include drawings from several films with caricatures, doodles, and Christmas cards mixed in. Wherever possible, the people who worked on each project, the approximate date(s) it was in production, and the reason for stopping work on it have been noted.

It's not always possible to establish these facts, but the solutions to some mysteries may still lie hidden in the studio archives or in the personal papers of the hundreds of artists who contributed to the extraordinary animated legacy of the Walt Disney Studio.

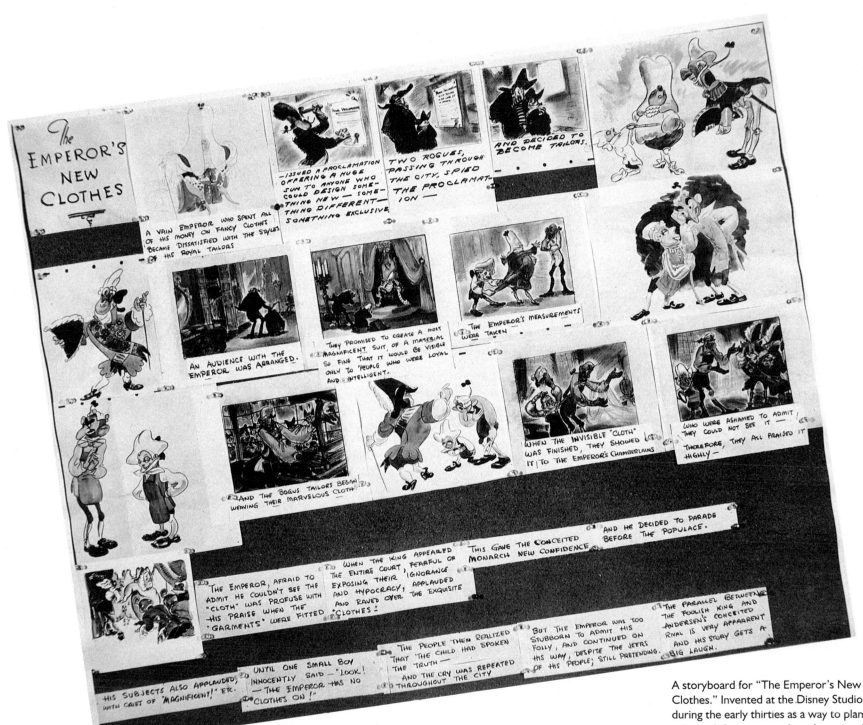

A storyboard for "The Emperor's New Clothes." Invented at the Disney Studio during the early thirties as a way to plan animated shorts, a storyboard consisted of a four-by-eight-foot panel of cork-board, on which the artists could pin sketches and captions. Photostats like the one shown here would be made for the director and key artists to work from when the film went into production.

I THE DISNEY STUDIO

"PRIMARILY A PLACE OF WONDER"

My role? Well, you know I was stumped one day when a little boy asked, "Do you draw Mickey Mouse?" I had to admit I did not draw anymore. "Then do you think up all the jokes and ideas?" "No," I said, "I don't do that." Finally he looked at me and said, "Mr. Disney, just what do you do?" "Well," I said, "sometimes I think of myself as a little bee. I go from one area of the studio to another and gather pollen and sort of stimulate everybody. I guess that's the job I do."
— Walt Disney

MARC DAVIS, one of the celebrated "nine old men" (a name Walt Disney gave his key group of animators and that echoed Franklin Roosevelt's description of the U.S. Supreme Court), described the Disney studio in its heyday as "primarily a place of wonder." The growth of that studio was neither smooth nor regular. Although Walt Disney experienced critical and financial triumphs, he also had to endure negative reviews and box-office losses. Three times during his career, he had to stake literally everything he had on the success of a single film.

Born on December 5, 1901, Disney showed an early talent for commercial art and began experimenting with animation while working for the Kansas City Film Ad Company in 1920. He and his friend Ub Iwerks taught themselves animation by studying E.G. Lutz's book *Animated Cartooning* and Eadweard Muybridge's photographs of humans and animals in motion. Together, they produced the "Newman Laugh-O-Grams," a series of one-minute topical cartoons for a Kansas City theater owner.

Two years later, Disney organized Laugh-O-Gram Films, with a staff that included Iwerks and Hugh Harman and Rudolf Ising, who later became cartoon producer/directors in Hollywood. The company made six films based on familiar fairy tales but failed to interest any of the major distributors. Disney decided to switch to films that combined live action and animation in 1923, and bankrupted his fledgling studio producing *Alice's Wonderland,* which featured a live-action little girl in a cartoon setting.

After joining his brother Roy in Los Angeles, Disney managed to interest distributor Margaret Winkler in a series based on *Alice's Wonderland.* Iwerks, Harman, and Ising soon joined Disney in Los Angeles, and the series ran through late 1926. Under pressure from Charles Mintz (Winkler's husband, who had taken over the business), Disney developed a new cartoon series starring Oswald the Lucky Rabbit. (Oswald was probably designed by Iwerks, who ranks as one of the foremost animators of the silent era; Disney had quit drawing to concentrate on production, organization, and story development.) Although Oswald made an unimpressive debut in *Poor Papa* (June 1927), the films rapidly

A cute lady worm crawls up to the lens of the transit and primps in the mirror-like surface of the lense.

Goofy unwittingly spies on an attractive caterpillar through the lens of his surveyor's transmit in "Ditch Diggers." Artist: Ches Cobb; medium: pencil, colored pencil.

Disney conceived of Mickey Mouse, the most successful character in the history of animation.

Disney often said that he took the character's original name (Mortimer) and cheerful nature from a pet mouse that had lived in his Kansas City studio. When his wife rejected the name Mortimer, the mouse was rechristened Mickey. Iwerks designed the character by using the many mice that had appeared in earlier silent cartoons and the Pat Sullivan Studio's popular Felix the Cat as models.

Disney had originally envisioned the Mickey films as a silent series, but distributors weren't impressed with the first two shorts, *Plane Crazy* and *The Gallopin' Gaucho*. Fortunately, Disney saw the potential the new sound film technology offered, and decided to synchronize the third Mickey cartoon to the songs "Steamboat Bill" and "Turkey in the Straw." He spent every cent he could raise to pay for the soundtrack (he even sold his car), and managed to book the film into the Colony Theater in New York City without a distributor.

Steamboat Willie premiered on November 18, 1928, to enthusiastic audiences and rave reviews. Remembering the mistakes he had made with Oswald, Disney insisted on remaining an independent producer who kept all the rights to his characters.

The success of *Steamboat Willie* enabled Disney to expand his staff and put the jaunty mouse in a series of cartoons that continued to delight viewers. When Carl Stalling, a friend from Kansas City who had composed the score to *Steamboat Willie*, suggested animating a graveyard frolic to Edvard Grieg's "March of the Dwarfs," Disney put the idea into production. *The Skeleton Dance* (1929) launched the "Silly Symphonies," Disney's second successful film series.

improved and were soon receiving favorable reviews.

Disney felt the cartoon industry was developing "rigor mortis" during the late twenties. Convinced that more time and money would enable him to make better films, he went to New York in February 1928 to ask Mintz to raise his price per film from $2,250 to $2,500. Mintz responded by demanding that Disney accept a cut to $1,800 or lose the rights to the Oswald character—and his studio. The distributor had persuaded all of Disney's artists except Iwerks to come to work for him.

Mintz's underhanded scheme profoundly altered not only the development of the Disney studio but the art of animation and the history of popular culture as well. Mintz went on to produce Oswald shorts for one year for Universal, whose management then gave the character to Walter Lantz, who continued the Oswald series through 1943. During the train ride back to Los Angeles,

Disney was still determined to improve the quality of his cartoons. He hired the best artists he could find, and paid bonuses for exceptional pieces of animation. Disney spent so much money on his films that they frequently took more than a year to earn back their costs. (The profits from Mickey Mouse merchandise helped to make up the difference.) During the thirties, he instituted an unprecedented training program for his staff that included lectures not only in anatomy, drawing, and animation but in acting, staging, character analysis, and story analysis. These efforts yielded results: His shorts were soon not only better animated but also better plotted and paced than the cartoons of other studios.

When Disney announced that he planned to produce a feature-length animated film, the idea was dismissed as foolhardy. During production, *Snow White and the Seven Dwarfs* was referred to as "Disney's Folly" in Hollywood, and Marc Davis recalls a neighbor telling him, "Nobody'll sit through an hour and a half of animation!" But it was actually a logical step forward for Disney's studio. Charlie Chaplin and the other film comedians Disney admired had all given up shorts for features. The potential profits were far greater, and distributors and theater owners treated feature films with more respect.

When *Snow White and the Seven Dwarfs* opened in 1937, it was a box-office phenomenon. The more than $8 million it earned (an unheard-of sum in 1937 to 1938) enabled Disney to build a showcase studio in Burbank and launch an ambitious schedule that included the release of a new feature every year. That vision failed during the 1940s for several reasons. The most significant cause was the outbreak of World War II in Europe, which cut off the foreign markets that had provided about forty percent of the studio's income, a loss that contributed substantially to the box-office failures of *Pinocchio* (1940), *Fantasia* (1940), and *Bambi* (1942).

Another important factor was the 1941 animators' strike. The unionization of the Hollywood cartoon industry was a long, harsh battle, and no-

Mickey sculpts the lower eyelashes of the Mt. Rushmore–esque head in "Mountain Carvers." Artist: unknown; medium: pencil, grease pencil.

where was it fought more bitterly than at the Disney studio. The studio had always been Walt's personal realm, and he felt obligated to protect the artists he referred to as "my boys." Many of the men at the studio felt that their personal relationship with Walt meant more than any contract. But as the number of employees at the studio passed a thousand, it became impossible for Disney to maintain close contact with everyone, even though promotions, bonuses, and raises continued to depend entirely on his favor. About one-third of the artists joined a strike that began on May 29, 1941. Disney was hurt and angered by what he regarded as a betrayal. The strike was eventually settled while Disney was in South America, but the divisions it created festered for decades.

During the war, the studio switched the majority of its production to military training films, most of them commissioned by the U.S. Navy. Al-

though his studio churned out thousands of training films, Disney also managed to produce a full slate of shorts each year and release five features: *Dumbo* (1941), *Bambi* (1942), *Saludos Amigos* (1943), *Victory Through Air Power* (1943), and *The Three Caballeros* (1945). The federal government's policy of budgeting military films at a small profit enabled Disney to pay off the debts he incurred when *Pinocchio*, *Fantasia*, and *Bambi* failed to duplicate the success of *Snow White and the Seven Dwarfs*. Although the war years were a trying time for Disney, his studio reported a net profit of $50,000 in 1945. By the end of the war, Disney was in better financial shape than he had been since the success of *Snow White*.

THE CHAOTIC FILMS OF THE TWENTIES

Walt Disney had an extraordinary sense of plot and pacing, which makes it easy to understand his impatience with the anarchic cartoons of the silent era. During the teens and twenties, animated shorts were created with a casualness modern audiences find inconceivable. Dick Huemer, who began his long animation career at the Raoul Barré Studio in 1916, recalled:

> We {the individual animators} were given a portion of the picture, over a very rough scenario. Very, very sketchy, no [story]boards like we have today, nothing like that. The scenario would probably be on a single sheet of paper, without any models, sketches, or anything; you made it up as you went along. You were given a part of the picture, and you did what you wanted. If it was a picture about ice-skating, you took a scene of somebody on ice skates, and you used your own gags, and made it all up… We'd spend an evening talking about…[a story idea]. And that's all it amounted to… Generally it was picking a theme… We'd say, "Let's do a Hawaiian picture" "Fine. I'll do the surf stuff, you do the canni-

Goofy and the Big Bad Wolf attempt a dance number for "Mickey's Follies." Artist: Ferdinand Horvath; medium: pencil, colored pencil.

A pastel sketch of some orchestra members illustrates the transition to "Claire de Lune" for the continuation of *Fantasia*. Artist: Sylvia Holland.

bals," or whatever else. Five animators would do it, and we'd do it all in a week.

This haphazard approach to animated film-making continued into the sound era at many studios. When Leo Salkin went to work for Walter Lantz at Universal in 1932, he discovered that there was no story department. The scenarios for Lantz's "Oswald Rabbit" series were just cobbled together:

> Walt essentially put the stories together with the contributions of a number of people who had shown an ability to think funny and to come up with gags for the films. The way it worked was this: First a subject was chosen—Oswald Camping Out or Oswald at the North Pole, or a take-off on King Kong, then a notice was put up on the bulletin board asking those interested to turn

in gags; this was followed by a story meeting.... Out of the nonsense Walt would select the stuff that could be made into a film: comedy bits, funny lines, gags.... We took a locale, an occupation, a situation, or the basic premise of a popular feature and did a lot of gags, strung them together, built in a chase, and got out in under seven minutes.

Not all the silent and early sound cartoons were bad; some of them hold up surprisingly well. But they were crude and poorly structured. The artists who made them hadn't learned how to stage and time a gag effectively, how to pace a film so that the humor built to a climax, or how to present a story with a beginning, a middle, and an end. Recalling the silent cartoons he worked on, Huemer added:

Two of inspirational artist Ferdinand Horvath's sketches of the nasty title character for "Streubel Peter." Medium: pencil, colored pencil.

SCENARIOS AND STORYBOARDS

Although no two Disney films seem to have followed the same path from idea to screen, by the early thirties a standard method of development was in place at the studio. The shorts and, in some cases, the features began as brief scenarios written by the staff of the so-called Character Model Department. Joe Grant, who headed the department for many years, describes it as Disney's "think tank." A promising scenario would be developed visually, sometimes by the person who wrote it, sometimes by another artist or artists. Depending on the nature of the project, the preliminary artwork might range from a handful of rough pencil sketches to a series of elaborate watercolor paintings.

Animation has special strengths and weaknesses that writers accustomed to live action may not understand: Dialogue, camera shots, and effects that work well in live action may appear awkward in an animated film and vice versa. In a letter to a would-be contributor dated December 20, 1940, Disney explained: "... even though I have not seen the story, I feel reasonably safe in saying that we would not be interested in it, because our work is of such a highly specialized nature that it is pretty difficult to adapt outside material, other than a basic story idea, to our medium."

Although a few of the writers and designers who initiated and began developing these ideas were women, the overwhelming majority were men. "At that time, women were really not encouraged to be anything except ink and paint girls," explains Davis. "There were a few women at the studio who qualified as story people, but it wasn't encouraged. Things were run like a monastery and a nunnery— the nunnery was the ink and paint department, and the big church was filled with the animators."

If the idea and preliminary art received Walt's approval, they would be expanded into a rough

They weren't funny actually. They really weren't. We got very few laughs.... We actually didn't consider the audience as much as we should have. We did things more or less to please ourselves. It was as though we were enjoying ourselves, doing what we liked, what *we* thought was funny. It was just not understandable to audiences, very often.

Although silent cartoons gradually became more sophisticated and pleasing to audiences during the late twenties and early thirties, Walt Disney remained dissatisfied with the state of the medium. His decision to give up animating to concentrate on story development led to what may have been his greatest personal contribution to the development of the animated film. Although he had little formal training in literature or narrative structure, Disney was a spellbinding storyteller, with an innate understanding of plot, characterization, and pacing. Disney insisted that his films tell real stories, while the meandering shorts of rival studios were often little more than strings of cartoon gags.

storyboard. The storyboard was initially devised at the Disney studio by Win Smith, Ub Iwerks's former assistant, as a tool for planning animated shorts. It consisted of a series of drawings and captions pinned to six-foot corkboard panels. Although rough scenarios with sketches had been used for earlier cartoons, *Three Little Pigs* (1933) was the first film to be completely storyboarded.

The storyboard enabled the artists to preview a film before the animation began and to establish visual rhythms, styles, and moods through the use of different shots, camera movements, colors, etc. As the drawings were pinned to cork, individual sketches could be shifted or replaced as the project developed. The storyboard proved so effective as a tool that it quickly spread throughout the animation industry. Today, all commercials and most live-action features are storyboarded during preproduction. (The storyboard also led the animators to create the sport of pushpin throwing: A deft touch was required to make a pin stick in the cork instead of bouncing off.)

The rough boards would be presented by the development crew to Walt; if he approved them, the artists would continue refining and presenting the material. A presentation meeting could be a thrilling success or a crushing failure, as Disney was a direct and outspoken critic. The power to decide whether or not to proceed with the development of a film, a sequence, or even an individual piece of business for a character rested with Walt. His presence dominated the studio during the thirties and early forties, when he often stayed late into the night, examining the artists' work. It was not unusual for an animator to arrive in the morning and find that a discarded drawing had been rescued from the wastebasket and pinned to his desk with a note from Walt telling him not to throw away "the good stuff."

"A story meeting was like a court trial—you

Chanticleer: A brooding Reynard plots his next scheme in a Parisian café. Artist: Marc Davis; medium: watercolor, pen and ink.

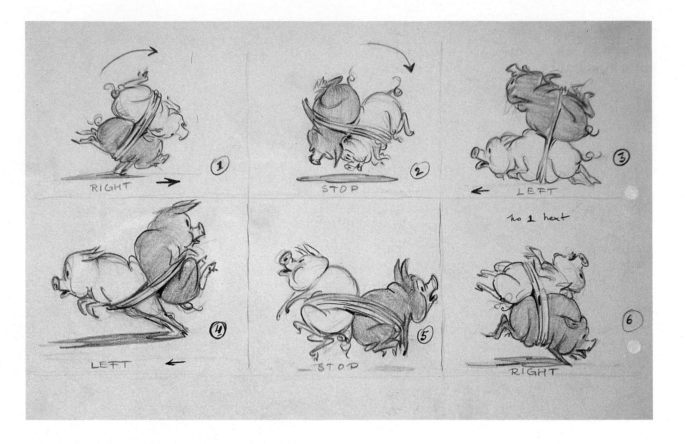

"Streubel Peter" ties two of his family's pigs together so they flip over each other. Artist: Ferdinand Horvath; medium: pencil, colored pencil.

were either going to be executed or receive a life sentence," says Grant. "It was a difficult experience to explain, because you had prepared material for a man who was supposedly going to look at it fresh. But that board had been there on Saturday and Sunday, when he had come in and memorized it. By the time you got in on Monday, he was way ahead of you. He was prowling that place seven days a week, and nights to boot.

"Walt had a couple of giveaways," Grant continues. "He'd look at a board, and the director and the story man would be explaining it with a pointer up here, and he'd be looking down there. And all the time he'd be tapping with these heavy fingertips—we always said they had calcium deposits burned into them from cigarettes—that made a hell of a racket. We all knew at this point that it was not going to be a successful meeting. They beat out a tattoo that was almost like Morse code: 'This no damned good!'"

Occasionally, the story artists grew impatient with Disney's habit of ignoring the presenter and reading the storyboards at his own pace. Frank Thomas and Ollie Johnston, two other members of the "nine old men," recall that Webb Smith started one meeting by asking Walt, "'Do you see this drawing up here?' Walt assured him that he did. Webb continued, 'And you see this drawing down here?' Walt grunted a reply, but his curiosity was piqued. Webb concluded, 'Well, when I'm talking about this sketch up here, I don't want you looking at this sketch down here.' Walt laughed, but deliberately looked everywhere except where Webb was pointing from then on."

However, if Disney felt that a project was going well, he might let the artists work on it for weeks or even months without interfering. Davis remembers that the preproduction crew for *Bambi* rarely saw him because he liked what they were doing. A phone call from Disney's secretary that Walt would like to have a meeting was the signal to get the mess off the floor and the drawings onto the boards.

As Disney remained the absolute arbiter of what was good and what was produced, the artists often tried to anticipate his reactions. Salkin, who left Lantz for the Disney studio during the thirties, remembers, "The standard line of anybody over you was 'Oh, God, Walt hates this stuff' or 'You know what Walt likes …' People were always trying to do what they thought Walt would approve of, and sometimes it would work, but just as frequently, it didn't."

Walt Disney was a complex man who relied on his intuitive reactions to assess the material presented to him. Bill Peet, regarded by many of the animators as the most talented story man in the studio, insisted that there were really three Walts, the dreamer, the realist, and the spoiler, and that before any meeting, it was a good idea to call the guard at the studio gate to find out which Walt had come in that morning.

"Associating with a genius—Disney—that was something," said Huemer. "It was frightening. No, it was stimulating to be around Disney. When he'd come into a room, the hair would stand up on the back of your neck—figuratively. He'd have that effect on you. You'd feel the presence. It was spooky."

Grant recalls that the artists on the story crews enjoyed a special rapport with Disney: "Walt was very easygoing with the story department because he was a part of it—he wasn't an animator, he was an idea man and a story man. Consequently, he was a little more sympathetic to our problems. He

Penelope flees from a sinister incarnation of the Grandfather Clock that carries her to other worlds. She tries to hold on to a character who personifies the wind. Artist: Mary Blair; medium: watercolor.

may have been a little rough here and there, but he knew he had to come up with an answer himself. With the animators in a sweatbox session, it was another story."

But Disney's blunt responses sometimes caused tempers to flare. The most famous reaction to Walt's criticism involved story man Harry Reeves, who presented a series of boards one day. Walt didn't like any of the material and, after tearing the ideas apart, left the room. In a fit of anger, Reeves put his foot through one of the corkboard panels. Walt apparently had second thoughts, as he walked back into the room—and found Reeves with his foot stuck through the board. Grant calls this episode "one of the great moments in the studio's history."

PICTURES, NOT WORDS

During story presentations, Disney quickly grew impatient with words and insisted that story ideas should be developed visually. All the artists who worked with him agree that a good drawing could excite Disney in ways that the most eloquent prose could not.

"The big contest was to inspire Walt, and the only way we could inspire him was graphically—not verbally," says Grant. "He would take off from a good drawing and a good idea. And each drawing had to have an idea in it that would inspire him—not just each sequence of drawings." Davis adds, "When you worked with Walt, you had to have something to show him. He lost patience when you didn't have any more presents for him to open, and then you'd better change the subject or you'd lose what you had just accomplished."

The notes from meetings held during the thirties reveal Disney's detailed responses to the preliminary visual material his artists presented. "Tanglefoot" was an unmade short involving Mickey, Goofy, and the title character, a somewhat

The unpleasant Landlord of the tailor shop run by Mickey, Donald, and Goofy in one version of "The Emperor's New Clothes." Artist: unknown; medium: pencil, watercolor.

recalcitrant racehorse. In a meeting held on April 22, 1938, Disney suggested, "Mickey could say, 'You put on the harness and get Tanglefoot in the sulky. I have to go over and pay my entry fee.' When he comes back, Tanglefoot is in the sulky and the Goof is in the harness. The Goof would say, 'Here we are … all ready.' When Mickey had given the Goof his instructions, the Goof could be dumbly puzzled and say, 'It don't sound right … but orders is orders.'"

Throughout the two-and-one-half-hour "Tanglefoot" meeting, Disney toyed with variations on that idea. His ability to concentrate on the details of this single cartoon seems incredible. In 1938, *Pinocchio* and *Fantasia* were in production, *Dumbo* and *Bambi* were in preproduction, and the studio released eighteen cartoon shorts, including three Academy Award nominees (*Good Scouts, Brave Little Tailor, Mother Goose Goes Hollywood*) and the Oscar-winning *Ferdinand the Bull*. Disney oversaw all these films—as well as a number of unproduced features and shorts.

In story meetings, Disney regularly stressed that the comedy in cartoons should come from the interaction of the characters' personalities rather than from simple sight gags. In another meeting on "Tanglefoot," he said, "We have to build up the personality of this guy [Tanglefoot] and get away from those gags like having his rear end pop down and all that…. Strive for the personality of the horse rather than rely on props for gags….You can hang everything around him instead of depending on an assortment of slapstick gags."

In the April 22 meeting, Disney and seven of his artists toyed with various ideas for more than two hours: Tanglefoot could sneeze and win by a nose; he might get confused, run backward, and win by a tail; as the owner of a rival horse, Black Pete might send him goldenrod to sabotage his chances. Goofy might bring the horse "good luck"

The beautifully detailed watercolor studies of the life of
Hans Christian Andersen prepared by the Disney artists
impressed coproducer Louis B. Mayer. Artist: unknown.

flowers that would trigger a fit of sneezing; Goofy could inadvertently dismantle the sulky while attempting to grease it. The other characters would provide the comedy; Mickey would respond to their actions.

In a meeting in mid-May, Disney expressed his reservations about the direction the story was taking—and repeated his concern that the best artists were too busy working on the features to provide the polished animation the cartoon would require:

> I am worried whether or not we have the animators that can put the personality into Tanglefoot and Mickey—or the Goof, for that matter. Without it, you're lost and you still have to work on the story. I feel we should get away from that old gag of the starter and the bell. There is more comedy in our characters…. Here, we're depending on gags that are so damn old they're on crutches. Like that gong—it's a shame we have to resort to that, when we can use things we see in everyday life—actions caricatured.

When Harry Reeves suggested that Goofy could hit himself in the head with a mallet and the mallet would sprout the bump rather than his head, Walt replied, "We've thrown that gag out a half dozen times. This time we'll say, 'And stay out!'"

"What made Walt so damned effective was that he really thought in terms of the characters in situations as acting and moving and living things," says Salkin. "If Walt said to me, 'Mickey wouldn't think this way …' Who knows how Mickey would think? But in Walt's mind, this is what Mickey would think or feel, and it was valid. Everything he did was rooted in terms of storytelling—whether acting out parts or doing gags."

Disney also realized that an emphasis on character would enable him to assign the shorts to younger and/or second-string artists, and reserve the top animators for the more subtle work in the financially critical features. In another meeting on

"Tanglefoot" held on May 13, 1938, Disney explained, "Animators of the caliber we have for this [type of story] are usually good on cute stuff with kittens or pups or chickens… Think of some cute gags and characters that we feel sure we can get good results on… If we want to get decent results from the animators, we have to keep them with characters they know and can get hot over." He made the same point earlier that year in a meeting about another unproduced cartoon, "Yukon Mickey/Donald": "Every short we put out has to be [built] around characters we have established and characters we know the animators can handle properly."

Disney's insistence on the need to use the "established" characters who made up his studio's repertory company didn't mean that he wanted to repeat situations or gags from other films. He often stated his dislike of sequels, and frequently dismissed an idea by saying the artists were "relying too much on old stuff." "Yukon Mickey/Donald" was eventually shelved because the story was too similar to that of another short.

But Disney would reuse an idea if the artists could find a way of making it seem new. In a discussion of "Pluto's Pal, Bobo," an unmade short about a baby elephant, held on November 14, 1939, Walt reassured director Frank Tashlin, "There's nothing wrong with using bees if we have something that is sort of fresh with bees, you know. Don't worry about old situations if we give them a new twist." He made a similar point the same day in a meeting about a proposed Donald short, "The Haunted House." Carl Myer and Bill Jones planned to scare the Duck by having the instruments in a ghost-town orchestra make sounds that would approximate human speech—an idea that appealed to Disney:

> The freshness of this is having all these things that *can't* talk, talk. It wouldn't hurt to have the old haunted house in there, because it has a fresh

This mood study for "The Emperor's Nightingale"
sequence of the Andersen biography evokes
the look of Chinese export porcelain. Artist:
unknown; medium: watercolor.

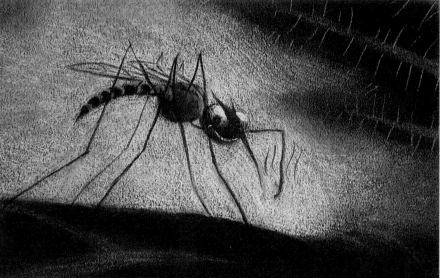

An innocent firefly and a fiendish mosquito from the proposed "Insect Ballet" sequence of *Fantasia*. Artist: Sylvia Holland; medium: pencil, charcoal, colored pencil, pastels.

idea in this sound. The thing to do is find out what we can make talk … try out some of these others [instruments] that they haven't tried. Get them all together and then begin to form some sort of story outline around that, working with the things we know will work … we have to turn this over to the director in a workable form. I'd like to turn it over to him with the sound all recorded."

He suggested that Myer and Jones spend a day in the studio sound-effects department to "see what can be done."

Disney frequently stressed the important role music could play in an animated film. Even before *Fantasia,* he was eager to blend animation and music, avoiding words altogether. During a meeting on "Tanglefoot" in 1938, he asked, "Couldn't we get something musical there and get away from all the dialogue? We don't need any excuse—just synchronize the action to the music. We are getting so far away from [the] little touches in our pictures that used to have a big appeal for people." Two years later, in a meeting on "The Elopement," a proposed Mickey short, Disney said:

I'd like to lay out the action to music and get this cute little score that goes running through the thing. It's the same way with Grandpappy when he comes out. That should be a musical break: The noise comes up and out comes this guy… Even his walk would be done to music … like a comic type of old man.

He took the concept even further in the discussions of "Pluto's Pal, Bobo," on November 20, 1939, when he suggested that composer Frank Churchill (who wrote the songs for *Snow White* and would later score several Disney features) create little themes for the characters that could be tied into a score.

Although he preferred to make the story points and delineate the characters through visuals whenever possible, Disney would sometimes suggest bringing one or two "dialogue men" onto a project. Frank Thomas and Ollie Johnston list four principal rules for dialogue in Disney animation: (1) Do not write dialogue that describes what you are seeing. (2) The words and the thoughts behind them should be unique to the specific character. (3) Dialogue must be written so that it offers something to animate. (4) Dialogue must be written so that the actor doing the voice can contribute something. But, they

"Streubel Peter" torments the chickens on his family's farm. Artist: Ferdinand Horvath; medium: pencil, colored pencil.

add, "Walt usually left out the dialogue until a sequence had been developed to the point where he could see how little was really needed. If the idea could be put over with an expression, an action, a sound effect, or with music, he would not use dialogue."

BUILDING A BETTER CARTOON

As development on a given film proceeded, a request for gags would circulate through the studio. The one-page notice would describe the theme of the film and ask the artists to submit ideas for jokes and pieces of animated business by a certain date. Anyone could enter, and the cleverest submissions that could be integrated into the fabric of the story earned bonuses of up to $10. "That was eating money in those days," observes Davis.

Artists who contributed exceptional material might be reassigned to the story department. Bill Peet recalls that he was moved to story on the basis of the drawings he submitted for a proposed "Bogyland" sequence in *Pinocchio,* a nightmarish counterpart to Pleasure Island. But joining the story department was not necessarily regarded as a step

up, as Salkin notes: "I'd been turning in gags, and Pinto [Colvig] asked if I'd be interested in working in story. I thought it was a terrible notion at first; I liked doing gags, but the key thing was to be an animator—anything else in the studio seemed largely secondary to that."

Toward the end of the development process, a director would be assigned to the film; he would also take part in the meetings. When Disney was finally pleased with the story, the director would take over and begin turning the boards into a film. After the boards were given to the director (or directors), their layout men, who plotted the physical path of the animated action in every scene, continued to develop the story.

"The directors always had to redo the storyboards to make them filmic," explains veteran story sketch artist Vance Gerry. "When you did the final layouts, ideally you would use what you did on the storyboards, but it didn't work that way very often. By the time you got to layout you did something entirely different—whatever the director wanted."

When the final storyboards and layouts were completed and approved by Walt, the dialogue, and sometimes the music, would be recorded. At this point, the animators would go to work and the film would begin to assume its final form. "Everything was kind of wide open until you had recorded the dialogue. Once it had been recorded, you were stuck with making what was there work," says Davis, "although it could be adapted visually."

The Disney animators were a singularly talented and hardworking group who had to bring everything in a film to life, devising gestures and expressions and individual styles of motion that expressed each character's personality. In live-action filmmaking, a director often benefits from happy accidents that occur when the light on the set shifts or an actor stumbles. In animation, every detail of every scene must be painstakingly drawn, examined, corrected, and redrawn. An animator and his assistants rarely produced more than a few seconds of footage per week, and Disney stressed quality over quantity. Grim Natwick, who was in charge of animating the Princess in *Snow White*, recalled redoing one scene fourteen times before he and Walt were satisfied.

Another tool invented at the Disney studio that soon played a key part in production was the pencil test: The animators' rough drawings were photographed on inexpensive black-and-white film stock, projected, and studied. This visual review enabled the animators to refine the timing and details of the motions to produce more polished results than the artists at other studios during the thirties, who just animated their scenes, flipped the drawings, and hoped for the best.

Disney also oversaw the animation process, reviewing the pencil tests with the animators and directors. Originally conducted on a Moviola in the small, stuffy space under a stairwell, these reviews were dubbed sweatbox sessions—a name that stuck even after they were shifted to air-conditioned projection rooms.

"Walt was the secret, he bounced around the whole production of a cartoon, down to the littlest things," comments animator Ward Kimball. "People don't realize the importance he had—down to deciding whether a character should look left or right or roll his eyes. Walt was the final editor on every damned scene."

When Disney was satisfied, the animators' drawings would be transferred to cels, colored by the women in the ink and paint department, and photographed against the backgrounds. Music and sound effects would be added, and the film would be released.

"As [a film] moved along, Walt never stopped improving it, polishing it," said Huemer. "That was the beauty of Walt's place. It was never finished until it was previewed. And even then it wasn't finished sometimes … Everybody thought Walt had some kind of deep, secret formula—things known only to him that made his cartoons so good…. The only trick he ever had was great genius and appreciation, and his perfectionism. Boy, he had it!"

THE END OF AN ERA

When World War II ended, Disney embarked on an ambitious program of feature production, but audiences failed to respond to his work as they had before the war. *Song of the South* earned a modest profit, but the three so-called package features (collections of short animated segments set to popular musical selections), *Make Mine Music* (1946), *Fun and Fancy Free* (1947), and *Melody Time* (1948), failed to generate much enthusiasm from critics and audiences. *The Adventures of Ichabod and Mr. Toad* (1949) received a similarly lackluster response.

Disney seemed to have lost touch with both the general audiences that had flocked to *Snow White* in record numbers and the intellectuals who had once praised his films ecstatically. Deeply in

debt, he decided to stake everything on one last full-length cartoon, and he chose *Cinderella* from the stories in development. The success of *Cinderella* (1950) saved Disney's studio, but it also marked a return to the style of storytelling he had pioneered in *Snow White*.

The failure of the boldly innovative *Fantasia* and more modestly inventive package features meant that he could no longer push the boundaries of animation as he had done during the thirties. Disney chafed at these restrictions and began to lose interest in the medium. The development process began to falter as fewer animated films were put into production.

Walt had other interests now. He started producing nature documentaries, beginning with the Oscar-winning *Seal Island* in 1948. He used several million dollars in frozen assets in England to enter the live-action market. *Treasure Island* (1950), his first feature, attracted little attention, but the success of *20,000 Leagues under the Sea* (1954) and *Davy Crockett, King of the Wild Frontier* (1955) established him as a serious live-action producer.

Disney also set out to realize his ambition of creating an amusement park and used the new medium of television to finance it. The *Disneyland* TV series debuted on October 17, 1954, on ABC, followed by *The Mickey Mouse Club* on October 3, 1955. Disneyland opened on July 17, 1955.

All these activities meant that Walt had less time and energy to devote to animation. In 1942, the studio released nineteen shorts; in 1954, the number fell to ten; and shorts were phased out of production in 1955–1956, except for occasional specials and featurettes. Not surprisingly, except for television projects, the number of films in development also continued to decline.

The veteran animators, led by the "nine old men" (Les Clark, Marc Davis, Ollie Johnston, Milt Kahl, Ward Kimball, Eric Larson, John Lounsbery,

The human army advances into battle beneath a gathering storm for "The Ride of the Valkyries" sequence developed for *Fantasia*. Artist: Kay Nielsen; medium: charcoal, pastels.

Kabibonokka, the North Wind, emerges "from his home among the icebergs" in a sketch for "Hiawatha." Artist: Dick Kelsey; medium: charcoal, pastels.

Opposite
A windmill begins to transform itself into a threatening Giant in the addled mind of Don Quixote. Artist: unknown; medium: pastels.

would excite people by how he would act things out or suggestions he would make.

"Even during *Sleeping Beauty,* there were problems, because Walt always wanted to oversee every aspect of it, and his time was taken up with Disneyland," adds animator/story man Burny Mattinson. "Consequently, it took a very, very long time to make the picture. He wasn't really there full-time, as he had been in the past, when you had more imagination being put into the films. I got the feeling that as Walt's interest was shifting to Disneyland, there was getting to be less and less imagination in the films. We were getting more redundant and doing things similar to what we had done."

As live-action production, television, and the park became the focus of the company, there were complaints that the animated features cost too much and took too long to produce. Some of the businesspeople urged Disney to discontinue them. He refused, but the artists were pressured to streamline the animation process, especially after *Sleeping Beauty* (1959)—which had taken four and half years to create—lost more than $1 million on its initial release. The familiar method of visually developing long sequences that might be shortened or cut from the finished film was now deemed too inefficient; for *101 Dalmatians,* Bill Peet wrote the first screenplay for a Disney animated feature, switching the narrative to the dogs' point of view.

"When I was working on the story, the girls in the ink and paint department were afraid that the studio wouldn't do another feature and that they'd be out of work," Peet recalls. "When they heard I was working on a picture about a woman who murders dogs and takes their skins, they got upset at the idea that we'd make that picture—they thought it was insane. They didn't know where the idea came from—I thought it was funny."

Peet also wrote the screenplay for *The Sword in the Stone* (1963) but left the studio during

Wolfgang Reitherman, and Frank Thomas), were left more and more to themselves to produce the features. It became harder to get Disney to come to meetings about animated films, although when he did appear, he was as enthusiastic and discerning as ever. Vance Gerry, who came to the studio in 1955, says:

> You wouldn't see him very often, but when you did, you got his full attention. He worked very closely with the characters: what they would do and what they would say. It was very easy for him to change his mind, but he was always looking for something better. If he was in the right mood, people would be very excited, and he

preproduction on *The Jungle Book*. Gerry remembers that his presence was missed in the story department, but the practice of scripting the animated features continued.

"We would send a script to Walt, and he would say yes or no," Gerry explains. "When we got the script down, we'd make the storyboards—which was absolutely the wrong way to do it. There were a number of people who thought animated cartoons should not be written, they should be *drawn*, and that's the way they should be developed. But, practically speaking, that was the way we had to work."

Disney's death on December 15, 1966, left an enormous and obvious gap. Although his studio continued to function, much of the originality went out of the films, both produced and unproduced. The animators seemed content to repeat themselves in *The Aristocats* (1970), *Robin Hood* (1973), and *The Fox and the Hound* (1981), although *The Rescuers* provided a rare, bright dose of imagination in 1977. Even the unmade films from this period—"Hansel and Gretel," "The Four Musicians of Bremen," "Scruffy"—seem uninspired and derivative. George Dunning's *Yellow Submarine* (1968) and Ralph Bakshi's *Fritz the Cat* (1972) suggested that the Disney studio had lost the aesthetic leadership of the animated feature.

Another factor contributing to the general sense of stagnation was the failure of the studio to recruit new artists. Because the Disney staff was regarded as the best in the world, everyone apparently assumed that the same men would go on making films forever—even after Walt's unexpected death. Very few animators were hired during the fifties and sixties, but between 1970 and 1977, twenty-five new artists were taken on, although about half of them departed when Don Bluth left to found his own studio in 1979. The release of *The Fox and the Hound* was pushed back, and the

A breaking wave assumes the form of a monster in Mel Shaw's preliminary drawing for the "Finlandia" section of "Musicana." Medium: pastels.

A sketch for a film identified only as "Miscellaneous Musical Idea" turns French horns into tropical fish. Artist: unknown; medium: pastels.

The shimmering dragonfly from the "Insect Ballet" echoes the iridescence of Art Nouveau ceramics. Artist: Sylvia Holland; medium: watercolor.

belated recruitment and training program continued, although major changes at the studio occurred before the young artists had a chance to make much of an impact.

During his lifetime, Disney had developed a rambling but ultimately centralized method of developing animated films. The problem with this system—which became obvious after his death—was that it required Walt or someone else with a unifying vision to oversee every aspect of production. As Gerry notes, "You had to have Walt or somebody like Walt to have a point of view. Now it was divided among all these workers, so the focus was diminished. Walt knew what he wanted, and that's why Walt Disney animation was successful: because he knew what he wanted—even before the animators were able to do it."

Without Walt to provide that vital focus, the artists seemed content to rework material that had proved successful in earlier films. Phil Harris's happy-go-lucky ne'er-do-well bear provided one of the highlights of *The Jungle Book,* so *The Aristocats* and *Robin Hood* also featured happy-go-lucky ne'er-do-well characters voiced by Harris. The Disney films from the seventies generally seem uninspired, but they sustained the animation division during a difficult time. Critics regularly declared that the animated feature was moribund, if not dead, and it seemed likely that animation production in America might soon be restricted to mindless kidvid TV shows. It required the energy and enthusiasm of a new team of artists and executives to reclaim Disney's vision and begin redefining what an animated feature could be.

II MICKEY, DONALD, AND GOOFY

The life and ventures of Mickey Mouse have been closely bound up with my own personal and professional life. It is understandable that I should have a sentimental attachment for the little personage who played so big a part in the course of Disney Productions and has been so happily accepted as an amusing friend wherever films are shown around the world. He still speaks for me and I speak for him.
    —Walt Disney

WALT DISNEY'S STUDIO was built on the success of *Steamboat Willie* and the subsequent Mickey Mouse shorts. No one had expected Mickey to prove so phenomenally popular, and the royalties from Mickey Mouse merchandise paid for the ambitious program of expansion and education that Disney launched in the early thirties. The Lionel Company was rescued from bankruptcy in 1934 by the sale of 235,000 tin toys of Mickey Mouse on a railroad handcar; more than 2.5 million Mickey Mouse watches were sold during the first two years they were offered.

Even Disney was surprised by the initial success of Mickey Mouse, although he often remarked, "I only hope that we never lose sight of one thing … that it all started with a mouse."

MICKEY MOUSE

After the premiere of *Steamboat Willie*, Disney signed a one-year distribution deal with Pat Powers, the inventor of the Cinephone system, which he had used to record its soundtrack. Powers apparently planned to use the Disney cartoons to publicize his system, then dump them. But within a year, Mickey had begun to rival Felix the Cat in popularity, and Powers tried to keep this increasingly lucrative property. He offered to buy the small but growing studio and pay Disney the impressive salary of $2,500 per week to run it. When Disney refused, Powers revealed that he had hired Ub Iwerks to create a new cartoon series. Disney was shocked to learn that his friend and partner for more than a decade had accepted the deal. After

Opposite
Goofy demonstrates his quick-draw technique in "How to Be a Cowboy." Artist: unknown; medium: pencil, colored pencil.

Donald Duck plays Sherlock Holmes as he attempts to trace the source of an epidemic in "Public Enemy No.1." Artist: unknown; medium: charcoal pencil.

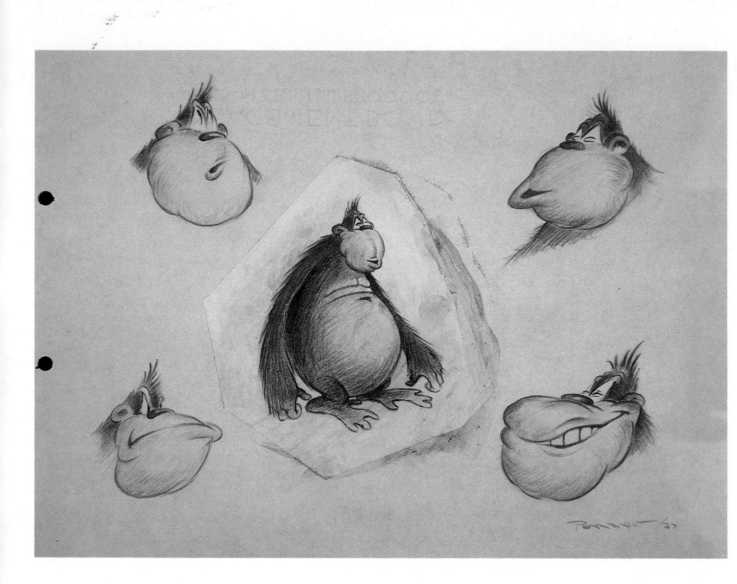

breaking with Powers, Disney signed a two-year distribution deal with Columbia Pictures.

(Iwerks sold his 20 percent interest in the studio back to Disney for $2,920 and went to work for Powers for $300 per week. Had he retained it, his interest in the Disney studio would have been worth about $2 billion by the mid-1990s. Although it never enjoyed any great success, Iwerks's studio stayed in business through 1940, when he went back to work for Disney, concentrating on special effects and technical innovations.)

Mickey's popularity continued to rise despite changes in distributors and personnel. Signs announcing "A Mickey Mouse Cartoon" appeared on theater marquees alongside the titles of the features during the thirties, and "What, no Mickey Mouse?" became a slang phrase for any disappointment. By 1932, over one million children had joined the first Mickey Mouse Club.

The best Mickey shorts were made during the mid-thirties, when animator Fred Moore redesigned the character, giving him his most endearing proportions. The rectangular feet, relatively small ears, and blobby black hands that had made Iwerks's original design for the character look rather blocky were softened into rounder forms that were both more

Erdman Penner's sketches of a gorilla for "Jungle Mickey" display the slightly goofy appeal that characterized late-thirties cartoons. Medium: colored pencil.

"Mickey's Toothache" would have depicted a surreal nightmare in which Mickey Mouse was tormented by dentists and monstrous versions of their instruments. Artist: unknown; medium: pencil, colored pencil.

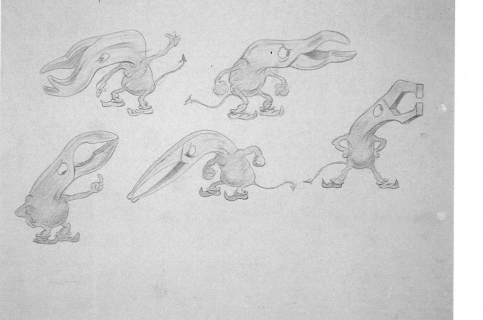

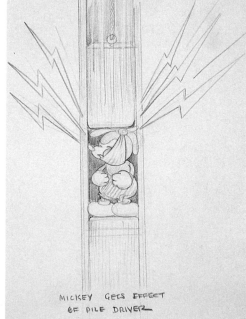

MICKEY GETS EFFECT OF PILE DRIVER

Production was suspended on "Pilgrim Mickey" in early 1939, although the artists felt the preliminary drawings displayed great promise. The gags involving Mickey and his nephews were submitted by Brian McIntyre; the artists received bonuses for good ideas. The mimeographed drawing appeared on a sheet requesting gags that circulated among the artists. An elaborately rendered pan background shows where Mickey will encounter an unfriendly warrior. Artist: unknown; medium: pencil, colored pencil.

appealing to audiences and easier to animate. His ears grew larger, and he was given the white gloves that made his hands and fingers distinguishable.

When a later generation of animators revived the character in *Mickey's Christmas Carol* (1983) and *The Prince and the Pauper* (1990), they sought to recapture the charm he had displayed in the mid-thirties, when he was principally animated by Moore, Frank Thomas, and John Lounsbery.

Although Mickey grew less mischievous during this period, he retained an irrepressible energy and resourcefulness. The artists played his boyish enthusiasm against fantastic settings in such classic films as *Thru the Mirror* (1936), *Brave Little Tailor* (1938), *Gulliver Mickey* (1934), and *The Band Concert* (1935), a pattern many of the unproduced shorts from this era follow. In the uncompleted "Sea Monster" (aka "Mickey's Sea Monster"), which was

Production was suspended on "Pilgrim Mickey" in early 1939, although the artists felt the preliminary drawings displayed great promise. The gags involving Mickey and his nephews were submitted by Brian McIntyre; the artists received bonuses for good ideas. The mimeographed drawing appeared on a sheet requesting gags that circulated among the artists. An elaborately rendered pan background shows where Mickey will encounter an unfriendly warrior. Artist: unknown; medium: charcoal, pastels, pencil, color pencil.

"PLUTO'S ROBOT TWIN"

HOWARD KAKUDA — DISNEY

D

C

5/17/38

Pink Pink Ponk

MICKEY OILS ROBOT FOR THE FINISHING TOUCH

CLANK PLINK CLANK

HELP PLUTO!

wanders through darkest Africa in "Jungle Mickey," which the artists worked on in the late spring of 1937. Ed Penner contributed some very funny pencil drawings of Mickey encountering a tribe of Ubangi-like natives. Some of the later versions of the story include Donald and Goofy.

Strangest of all these fantasy adventures was "Mickey's Toothache," which the artists worked on from April through October 1938. Under the influence of laughing gas, Mickey enters a nightmarish world inhabited by living teeth, an anthropomorphized spool of dental floss, toothbrush monsters, and bizarre creatures that are half animal/half dental pliers. Mickey is hauled into a courtroom where a judge with a wisdom tooth for a head tries him on the charge of "teeth neglect." The preliminary drawings suggest that the film could have rivaled the "Pink Elephants on Parade" number in *Dumbo* and the title song from *The Three Caballeros* for no-holds-barred surrealism. Unfortunately, no notes survive to indicate why this film was never put into production.

After the success of *Snow White and the Seven Dwarfs,* animated features occupied most of Disney's time and energy (and received most of the attention in the press), but he continued to produce shorts. Disney still attended story meetings and kept a close watch on every film. At times, he seemed to chafe at the limits feature production imposed on the shorts. In a meeting with Frank Tashlin and Bill Jones on the Donald Duck cartoon "Museum Keeper" in November 1939, he complained that he couldn't spare the animators needed to draw a lot of minor characters in the film:

> Oh, hell, I have that "Concert Feature." We have to keep those things rolling out. If we don't get

developed during the summer of 1935, Mickey, Donald, and Goofy confront a comic sea serpent. Several artists offered design ideas for the monster, and some of these odd-looking beasts seem to anticipate the look of Dr. Seuss's fantastic menageries. The drawings have the appealingly clunky look of thirties cartoons and suggest that "Sea Monster" could have been a winning short.

In "Hillbilly," which began development in November 1934, Mickey inadvertently arouses the ire of shotgun-toting moonshiner Black Pete, who mistakes him for a "revenoor." Mickey later attends a country dance, where he meets a cute hillbilly version of Minnie. The sheet requesting gag ideas notes that "plot is still open—suggest a simple story to tie the atmosphere, entertainment, and fight together." As a newsreel photographer, Mickey

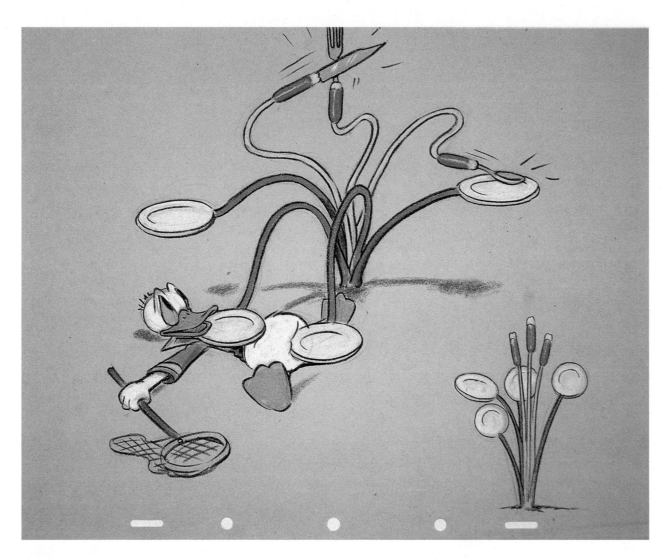

DON OKTAPAULTS CUT
OF SCENE INTO
ANOTHER TRAP

BWROING

LA LOCA MARIPOSA
CAUGHT BY
Donald Duck

Pluto is less than delighted with
the mechanical counterpart his owner
has devised in these preliminary
drawings for "Pluto's Robot Twin."
But when the automaton dog attacks
Mickey, Pluto comes to the rescue.
Artist: Howard Kakudce; medium:
pencil, red pencil.

In "La Loca Mariposa" ("The Crazy
Butterfly"), Donald Duck would have
portrayed a butterfly collector in
a remote South American jungle.
Donald is attacked by a bizarre duck-
eating plant. With mounting frustration,
he attempts to free his derriere from
a small bird cage. The final image in
the film would have been Donald,
mounted like an insect specimen.
Artist: unknown; medium: charcoal,
pastels, pencil, colored pencil.

a feature out there every so often, we're going to go broke. They must come out.... We will be able to make some good shorts if we stick to the things we can do. If we could get a simple line on this.

Although he remained popular as a character, Mickey Mouse appeared in fewer and fewer cartoons during the late thirties and forties. Of the fourteen shorts released in 1940, only three featured Mickey: In *Tugboat Mickey,* he appeared with Donald and Goofy; in *Pluto's Dream House* and *Mr. Mouse Takes a Trip,* he served as a foil for Pluto.

Ironically, Mickey was the victim of his own popularity. In an effort to please his many fans (and their parents), the artists gradually transformed the rowdy scamp of *Steamboat Willie* into a polite, well-behaved nice guy who acted as the straight man for the funnier and more flexible Donald, Goofy, and Pluto. Disney summed up the problem in an interview with Irving Wallace in *Collier's* in 1949: "Mickey's decline was due to his heroic nature. He grew into such a legend that we couldn't gag around with him. He acquired as many taboos as a Western hero—no smoking, no drinking, no violence."

As the character limitations on Mickey grew stricter, it became increasingly difficult to find ideas for him that were funny. Stories that didn't require him to do anything untoward often lacked the sharp conflicts necessary for cartoon comedy. In a meeting on the Mickey-Donald-Goofy short *Mountain Carvers* in August 1939, Disney noted that a series of gags involving a pesky woodpecker would be funnier for Donald Duck than for Mickey:

> ... Mickey isn't funny in a situation of that sort. I think people think of Mickey as a cute character—he is a cute character—and he should be more likable in everything he does. I have always kind of compared Mickey to Harold Lloyd—he has to have situations [or] he isn't funny.... I'd rather not make Mickey [films] if we don't get the right idea for him.

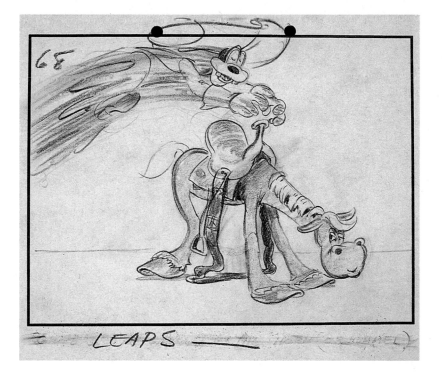

The notes and preliminary drawings for several uncompleted shorts reveal just how hard it became to devise the kinds of situations Disney felt Mickey needed. Instead of being the one who initiates the action, Mickey was increasingly relegated to the role of a character who reacts to what others do—or just looks on.

"Pilgrim Mickey," which underwent extensive preproduction work in 1938–1939, illustrates his transformation from active hero to passive observer. The film was to open with a shot of a settler's cabin; inside, Mickey appears to be wrestling with an Indian chief in a warbonnet, but he's actually just using a feather duster to illustrate the tale he's telling his nephews. When he goes hunting, he mistakes an Indian's headdress for a turkey's tail and gets captured. Significantly, his nephews rescue him. In *Brave Little Tailor* and *Thru the Mirror*, he had been perfectly capable of overcoming his adversaries without help. A memo from Carl Nater, a Disney executive, dated April 4, 1939, reads, "We are sus-

pending this picture temporarily. There is no question in my mind but that we will, at a later date, put this picture back into production," but it was never completed.

For "Tanglefoot," which remained in development for most of 1938, the artists worked around Mickey—even though he was ostensibly the star of the film. The cartoon is set at a racetrack, with Mickey as the owner of a horse with hay fever. In a meeting on April 22, 1938, Disney and seven of his artists toyed with various ideas for more than two hours. But all their ideas had other characters providing the comedy; Mickey would merely respond to their actions.

The story artists never developed "Tanglefoot" to a point that pleased Disney, and the film was eventually shelved. But the problem of what Mickey's role should be in a cartoon persisted. In "Mickey's Nephews," an unmade short from 1938, he plays Santa Claus for a crowd of identical little mice similar to the ones who appeared

"How to Be a Cowboy": Goofy attempts to roll a cigarette and ends up smoking his glove. A bow-legged cowboy requires a special door. Goofy leaps into the saddle— with predictably disastrous results. Artist: unknown; medium: pencil, colored pencil.

HE EES VARY CLEVER – AND AS FOR GERONIMO – HA!
SHE IS IN ZEE BAG.

in *Orphan's Benefit* (1934). In "Men in Uniform" (developed in 1940), he's a milkman who provides a foil for a kitten reminiscent of Figaro in *Pinocchio*.

The story ideas grew even less interesting after the war, when Mickey was often reduced to an amiable suburban householder in the Ozzie Nelson mold. Mickey is relegated to a supporting role in "Talking Dog," a short developed in 1951. Pluto gets tricked into joining a sideshow by a crooked ventriloquist who looks a bit like Black Pete. Pluto soon tires of his bogus career, but Mickey does little more than offer him a chance to come home—a far cry from the intrepid character who entered an eerie castle to save Pluto in *The Mad Doctor* (1933).

Although its premise seems flimsy, under Milt Schaffer's direction, "Talking Dog" was almost completely animated. Fred Moore and Norm Ferguson, who had helped to develop Mickey and Pluto, did many of the key scenes. Although Moore animated a nice sequence of Mickey laughing and Ferguson contributed some clever animation of Pluto attempting to impress Mickey by walking on

his forepaws like a circus dog, both artists were clearly past their prime.

PLUTO

Pluto began his career as a pair of anonymous twin bloodhounds in *The Chain Gang* (1930); Disney felt Ferguson's handling of their expressions (especially the way they sniffed) warranted further development. The character reappeared as Minnie's dog, Rover, in *The Picnic* (1930); *The Moose Hunt* (1931) established him as Mickey's pet, and his name had become Pluto. However, it was Ferguson's celebrated animation of Pluto struggling with a sheet of flypaper in *Playful Pluto* (1934) that set his character.

Although Pluto and Mickey made an effective team in such excellent shorts as *The Pointer* (1939), most of the proposed Pluto shorts follow one of two basic patterns. He either encounters a strange animal or object, which gives the animators a chance to work with reactions modeled after the flypaper scene, or he meets an adorable new character who tries his patience and/or arouses his

jealousy, a formula introduced in *Mickey's Pal Pluto* (1933), remade as the Oscar-winning *Lend a Paw* in 1941.

In early 1938, Disney decided to bring back Bobo, the title character of *Mickey's Elephant* (1936). Pluto's jealous response to the endearing little pachyderm had provided many of the gags in that film, and the artists planned to reuse the theme in a short tentatively titled "Spring Cleaning." In a meeting on February 24, 1938, Disney complained that they hadn't "gotten" the character of Bobo yet; he felt the storyboard was "too disconnected and the stuff is not strong enough. There is a possibility for some cute stuff, but we've got to strengthen it."

The artists considered having Mickey, Bobo, and Pluto wreak havoc on Minnie's house as they attempt to clean it or having Mickey build a howdah for Bobo with the elephant and Pluto assisting, but the story failed to gel. A gag-request sheet for "Spring Cleaning" issued on July 22, 1938, stated that "no definite story plot has been developed as yet, and what is really needed is a good unusual, basic situation out of which a story can be

built." The film was shelved for over a year, then revived as a possible project for director Frank Tashlin as "Pluto's Pal, Bobo."

In a story meeting held on November 14, 1939, Tashlin complained, "I didn't get a lift from that housecleaning thing. It seemed so proppy and so gaggy." "It didn't go very far," Disney conceded. Pluto's resentment of Mickey's paying attention to Bobo became the central theme of the story, with a lot of gags about Bobo imitating Pluto and sucking things up with his trunk. At a meeting held six days later, Disney suggested putting Frank Churchill and Paul Smith to work on a score, and spoke enthusiastically about the film's possibilities:

> I know Fergy [Norm Ferguson] would be good on this little elephant. The boys he has with him are good on this kind of thing; this good, broad stuff. They are working on elephants now, anyway, on that other thing [*Dumbo*]. There's a lot of cute stuff there. I would rather see us working on a lot of that than I would too much slapstick … here you want to go for those little cute things; build the personality of the characters.

The film was shelved a second time, possibly

Donald's glove rolls a cigarette for him and lights it in a series of drawings for "Old Geronimo." Artist: unknown; medium: charcoal pencil.

THE GOOF PULLS UP THE TRI-POD WITH A SHOW OF EXPERTNESS — AND BEGINS TO SIGHT THROUGH THE INSTRUMENT WHICH BEGINS TO SAG DOWN — GOOF KEEPS LOOKING — FOLLOWING THE TRANSIT DOWN UNTIL HE IS FLAT ON THE GROUND WITHOUT KNOWING IT.

who presides over the household in the Tom and Jerry films. (A similar maid appeared in Disney's 1935 short *Three Orphan Kittens,* but the character was a regular feature of the MGM cartoons.) When she discovers the real source of the breakage, she praises Pluto as "a good samaritan"; he blushes, the puppy does a winsome take, and the film ends.

"The Good Samaritan" went in and out of production during 1943–44. A memo dated June 5, 1943, notes that $1,000 had been spent on cartoon materials and supplies, $2,001.94 on overhead, and $2,552.21 from a "reserve for abandoned stories," for a total of $5,554.15—a considerable sum at the time. The film was canceled six days later "at Walt's suggestion" but was revived in the fall of 1944. Clyde "Gerry" Geronimi was slated to direct, and three of the studio's top animators, Ollie Johnston, Ward Kimball, and John Lounsbery, did scenes before "The Good Samaritan" was finally shelved on August 14, 1944.

"Pluto's Robot Twin," a short developed by

because of Tashlin's departure from the studio. It was revived a decade later by director Jack Hannah, and some animation was completed before the project was finally abandoned in late 1949.

Another unfinished cartoon in which Pluto encounters an endearing little character is "The Good Samaritan," a film that combines elements of *Lend a Paw* and MGM's popular Tom and Jerry series. Pluto rescues a sad-eyed little puppy who's been left in the snow. The pup proceeds to break things as Pluto tries to clean the house, which gets him in trouble with a black housekeeper who resembles Mammy Two-Shoes, the formidable maid

George Stallings and Roy Williams in the spring of 1938, offers an example of a story centered on Pluto's reactions to an alien presence. Mickey builds a remote-controlled mechanical dog and uses it to tease Pluto. But the robot goes out of control, chasing Pluto and then Mickey. Just as the metal jaws are about to clamp down on his master, Pluto charges to the rescue. When the dust finally settles, Mickey is relieved to discover that the real Pluto has emerged victorious. He promises never to fool his pet again as Pluto disdainfully scratches dirt over the shattered remains of the robot.

Although the story sketches suggest some interesting visual contrasts between the movements of the living and mechanical dogs, Disney was not impressed. In a story session on May 25, 1938, he commented, "I don't know what the hell it is, but I personally can't get any lift out of it. Maybe there's something lacking in the robot dog. Maybe we're assuming too much … thinking that [these] things would be funny." After explaining that he would prefer a "story where Mickey could be cute—some situations and gags in them," he concluded, "I would rather have fewer and better pictures go through than worry about filling the quota."

THE DUCK

In his 1949 *Collier's* article, Irving Wallace quoted an unidentified studio writer as saying, "Mickey is limited today because public idealization has turned him into a Boy Scout. Every time we put him into a trick, a temper, a joke, thousands of people would belabor us with nasty letters. That's what made Donald Duck so easy. He was our outlet. We could use all the ideas for him that we couldn't use on Mickey. Donald became our ham, a mean, irascible little buzzard. Everyone knew he was bad and didn't give a damn. So we can whip out three Donald Duck stories in the time it takes us to work out one for the Mouse."

The 1931 book *The Adventures of Mickey Mouse* included Donald's name as one of Mickey's friends, but the character didn't make his screen debut until three years later in *The Wise Little Hen* (1934). Clarence Nash had originally created Donald's signature nasal voice as a boy: It was an imitation of his pet baby goat. When Disney heard Nash for the first time, he reportedly cried, "That's our duck!"

Donald (or the Duck, as the animators always called him) soon became the most popular of

Goofy wrestles with a recalcitrant surveyor's transmit in "Ditch Diggers." A pretty caterpillar who winds up on the wrong end of his telescope gives him the cold shoulder. Artist: Ches Cobb; medium: pencil, colored pencil.

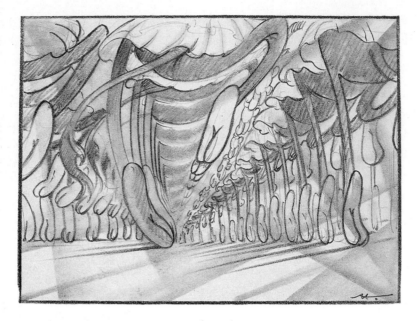

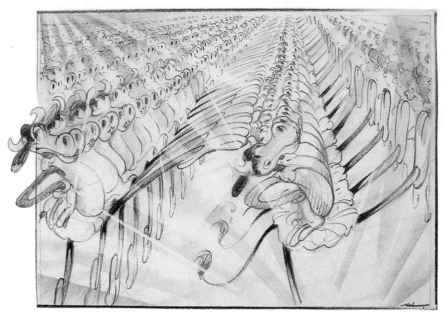

Ferdinand Horvath uses a chorus of Clarabelles to spoof Busby Berkeley's elaborate musical production numbers for "Mickey's Follies." Pluto chases a performing seal into the pool where the cow dancers are re-enacting "By a Waterfall" from *Footlight Parade*. Medium: pencil, blue pencil.

the Disney characters. Cartoons that began as vehicles for Mickey were often changed to Donald shorts. (In some cases, two versions of the storyboards survive: The boards for "Yukon Mickey/Donald," a cartoon developed in early 1938, show both characters in the same poses.) The volatile duck could be played against almost any situation because his temper would quickly bring him into conflicts that offered comic possibilities. In a 1939 sweatbox session on "Mountain Carvers," Disney commented, "The Duck is funny—you can just have the Duck walk along and get a laugh. The Duck can make damn near any kind of entrance and get a laugh."

Of all the Disney characters, the Duck changed the least over the years. During the mid-thirties, the physical appearance of the squat, long-billed bird in the sailor suit was reworked to make him rounder and cuter (and easier to draw). But when Donald threw his first tantrum later, in 1934 in *Orphan's Benefit,* his personality assumed its essential form. His impatience, greed, flash-pan temper, and unshakable faith in his ability to solve any problem (despite a wealth of evidence to the contrary) made him funny—and painfully human. If

Mickey became too nice a figure for an audience to identify with, Donald exhibited character flaws that the viewer might have but preferred to hide.

Donald could be funny on his own or as a foil: as Daisy's suitor, as the boob guardian of his three nephews, or as the outmatched foe of Chip and Dale, Spike the Bee, Humphrey the Bear, or the various opponents who appeared in one-shot cartoons. But he was funniest when he created problems for himself. The resourceful Mickey outwits his foes; Donald tries to outsmart other characters and ends up outsmarting himself. As Disney noted, "Don can be conceited and cocky, but he should always build up to a fall, so that things kind of kick back on him."

On April 15, 1938, story director Carl Barks sent around a preliminary outline and request for gags for the short "Donald Munchausen." Donald dismisses the adventure book he finds his nephews reading as "kid stuff" and spins a fantastic yarn about his feats of derring-do in a "strange, goofy valley in the crater of an extinct volcano" in Africa. There he meets living dinosaurs and King Kong, whom he beats in a contest of strength. Marc Davis submitted vivid sketches of the match between Donald

PLUTO CHASES SEALS INTO TANK, FILLED WITH
BATHING BEAUTIES.

Above: Horvath devised an aerial shot for "Mickey's Follies" even Busby Berkeley couldn't match. Clarabelle and her Cow Ballet give new meaning to the term "toe dancing." Artist: Ferdinand Horvath; medium: pencil, colored pencil, watercolor.

and Kong, earning a bonus of $7.50.

Raymond Jacobs received the same sum for a series of drawings about an encounter with "a cannibal tribe of savage 'Ubangi ducks,'" whose shields bear a sort of duck-billed skull. Although vastly outnumbered, Donald overcomes the tribe and uses the king's distended lower lip as a griddle on which to cook pancakes. One of the nephews ends this tall tale by making the shadow of Kong's hand on a wall, which sends Donald diving for cover.

The film had great potential, but it required a narrator, and Donald's all-but-incomprehensible voice simply couldn't carry such a complicated story. Barks's treatment of the characters and plot foreshadows the comic adventure stories he devised for the postwar Disney comic books, which feature extensive dialogue.

In "Museum Keepers" (also called "Old Masters" and "Donald and the Old Masters"), a short that was being developed for director Frank Tashlin in late 1939, Donald has to guard a priceless exhibit of rare paintings. The pictures are spoofs of famous canvases with the Duck taking the place of the original subjects. In a meeting held on November 2, Tashlin told Disney he felt that this cartoon could stimulate the public's interest in fine art in the same way that *Fantasia* was going to increase their appreciation of classical music. Disney, however, was more excited about using the paintings to publicize the film:

> If we could get them reproduced in *Life,* it would do more good than putting them in a book. You get to three or four million people that way, then you put your book out afterward. And you could make reproductions—Courvoisier makes good reproductions. I'd like to have a set myself for a den or something. A lot of people would be crazy to get them. The ones that holler bloody murder, we don't give a damn about them. The controversy is swell publicity. The public at large is going to get a big kick out of it.

A week later, Disney and Tashlin had another meeting on "Museum Keepers." They discussed the film's possibilities with obvious enthusiasm, but Disney objected to the number of critics and viewers Tashlin wanted to add, saying that he didn't have enough artists available to draw them. (In the previous meeting, Tashlin had pointed out that the film could be made relatively cheaply because the still images of the paintings would take the place of more expensive animation.)

At the end of the meeting, Disney decided to delay putting the story into production:

> We can animate it, but I'm afraid it won't look good. It will fall down. When we get the story together and ready, I'd like to feel it is animation proof. I think it's a funny idea if we can just get it worked out … I don't want to depend on just flashing these pictures at them. There has to be something behind the whole thing. I'd like to think on it a little bit.

"Museum Keepers" was never animated, but the Duck spoofs of famous paintings were used later in various print stories.

"La Loca Mariposa," a short planned in June 1944, repeats the South American setting and surreal actions of *Saludos Amigos* and *The Three Caballeros.* As a lepidopterist, Donald visits the mythical country of Venenuzela, "small in size but great in resources." He pursues butterflies with hands, baseballs, false teeth, shoes, and buttocks for wings. The Time Flies (whose round wings bear clock faces that make them look like open pocket watches) and other weird bugs anticipate the "Looking Glass Insects" sequence in *Alice in Wonderland.* Wilfred Jackson planned to direct this bizarre cartoon that concludes with Donald mounted on a board, like a specimen in a collection.

As Disney became increasingly interested in other projects after the war, it became difficult to find good material even for Donald, as "Share and Share Alike," a cartoon developed in 1946, reveals. The rough, scribbly storyboard for this film centers on a squabble between Donald and his nephews over an apple. Most of the film was animated, at a cost of over $26,000. But a preliminary screening for studio employees was apparently disastrous. The memo that announces the suspension of the production includes the note, "If drastic revisions are not made, 'Share and Share Alike' will be one of the worst cartoons produced by Disney."

GOOFY

In Rob Reiner's 1986 film *Stand by Me,* one of the juvenile characters asks, "If Mickey is a mouse and Donald is a duck, what's Goofy?" The correct answer is a dog. The Goof, as the artists called him, began life as Dippy Dawg, a bewhiskered hick in the audience in *Mickey's Revue* (1932). The animators agree that it was Dippy's odd, drawn-out laugh (sup-

plied by animator Pinto Colvig) that made him entertaining enough to use in other cartoons. His name was changed to Goofy for *Orphan's Benefit* (1934).

During the mid-thirties, animator Art Babbitt transformed the rubbery-limbed Dippy into the familiar, genial dim bulb. Babbitt described him as "a composite of an everlasting optimist, a gullible Good Samaritan, a half-wit, a shiftless, good-natured hick … Yet the Goof is not the type of half-wit that is to be pitied. He doesn't dribble, drool, or shriek." Goofy never seemed cretinous, but his blithe stupidity provided broad slapstick comedy in *Moving Day* (1936), *Clock Cleaners* (1937), *Lonesome Ghosts* (1937), and other cartoons.

Despite Goofy's popularity, in a meeting held on November 9, 1939, Disney expressed reservations about using the character. After noting that several stories for Donald were being developed, and that the studio hadn't done a Mickey and Minnie short in a while, he said, "I'd like to lay off the Goof. I don't think I have the men to do him. The best stuff we ever had was the Goof and the surfboard. The Goof and the piano was good, but we worked like a bunch of dogs to get it. Babbitt did it, but we really worked."

Although *Goofy and Wilbur* had launched the character's solo career eight months earlier, it was the "How to Ride a Horse" sequence in *The Reluctant Dragon* (1941) that redefined his personality and initiated a series of short cartoons that under the direction of Jack Kinney continued for more than a decade. While narrator John McLeish discusses the particulars of a sport, Goofy attempts to demonstrate each point in mime. As he's more enthusiastic than coordinated, the result is chaos. This new version of Goofy in these shorts, animated by John Sibley and Wolfgang "Woolie" Reitherman (who did the surfing sequence in the 1937 short *Hawaiian Holiday* that Disney praised), was eager, enthusiastic—and supremely maladroit. He was a

Opposite
Another surreal number for the cow-dancers in "Mickey's Follies."
Artist: Ferdinand Horvath; medium: pencil, colored pencil, watercolor.

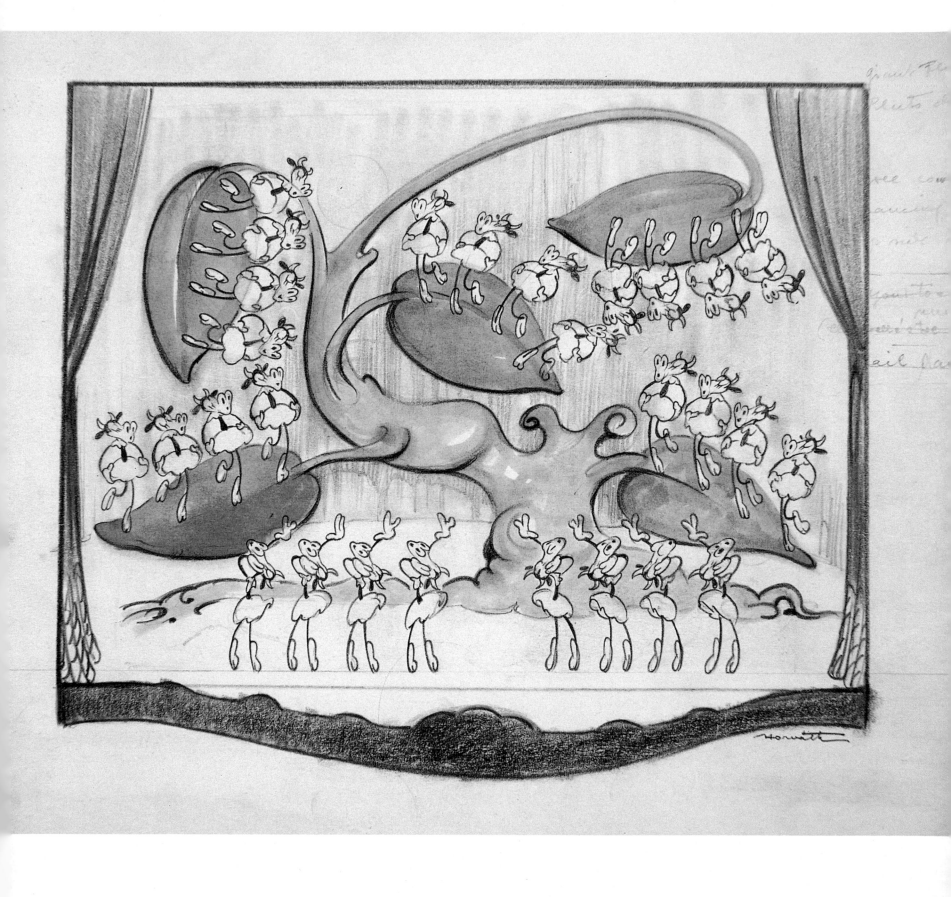

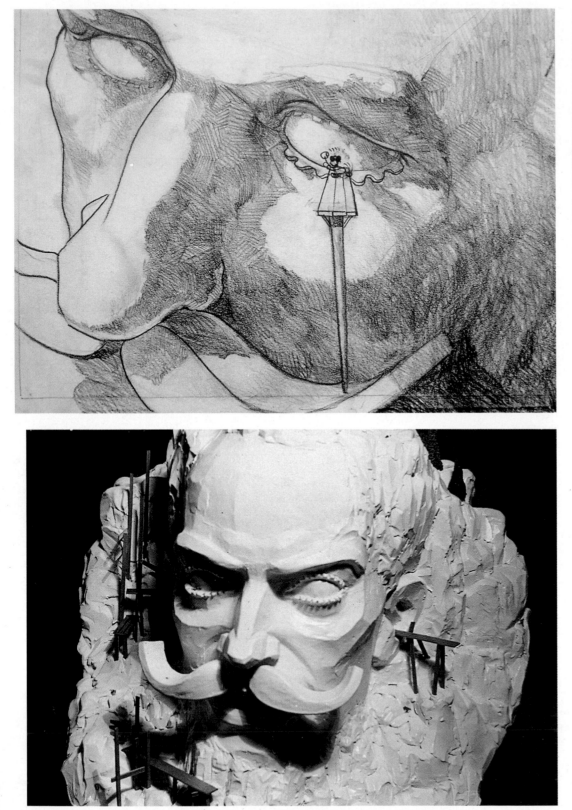

bit brighter than Babbitt's amiable thick wit, but much clumsier.

Undated preliminary drawings survive for at least two additional entries in the series. In "How to Be a Cowboy," Goofy appears as the chief wrangler on a dude ranch. He's so bowlegged, he has to enter through a specially cut door that flares at the bottom. After mistakenly rolling—and lighting—his glove instead of a cigarette, the Goof tries to bulldog a steer, which precipitates a string of slapstick gags about his getting dragged, kicked, bucked, and hog-tied. Goofy attempts to teach Pluto some new tricks in "How to Train a Dog," but Pluto proves to be a recalcitrant pupil, and the Goof ends up in the washtub of water he intended for Pluto's bath.

Both of these shorts offer some potentially amusing moments, but neither film has much of a story, and the gags look very familiar. Similar situations and jokes had appeared in other cartoons (including some from other studios), which may be why they were never produced.

The artists apparently liked the idea of Goofy playing a cowboy, as they explored the idea in an-

To help plan the film, artists sculpted a model of the monumental head for "Mountain Carvers." Predictably hiring Mickey, Donald, and Goofy to sculpt a mountainside would have proven disastrous. The front page of a newspaper would have been the opening image in "Mountain Carvers." Artist: unknown; medium; pencil, grease pencil, pen, newsprint, clay.

other postwar short, "Old Geronimo"—which had originally been planned as a Donald Duck cartoon with the alternate title of "Cow Poke Donald." A narrator introduces the hero in Mexican dialect: "I wawn you to meet my goot fran Tex—and he is out to capture the ruffest, tuffest steer een the whole state of Texas, Old Geronimo."

In the storyboard drawings, Donald rolls a cigarette with elaborate nonchalance and gets caught up in a lot of slapstick gags when he tries to rope the title character, a wily longhorn. Geronimo is crushed when his horns get broken off, so Donald reaffixes them with a sort of handlebar contraption. The film ends happily with the Duck playing the guitar as he rides the grateful Geronimo through the moonlit desert. But in the layout drawings, it's Goofy who rolls the cigarette, greets a coyote, and tries to rope the steer. Some animation, including the cigarette-rolling sequence, was completed before the film was shelved on January 30, 1947.

During the fifties, the Goof underwent yet another transformation. His IQ rose, his posture improved, his buckteeth disappeared, and in some films he even lost his floppy ears. Like Mickey, this Goofy was a middle-American suburbanite; in *Fathers Are People* (1951) and similar cartoons, he acquired a wife and a son. Animator Ward Kimball observes, "Goofy became our resident Homo sapien—with a dog face; our man who represented the common humanoid."

Decades later, a new generation of artists planned to star Goofy as a comic Tarzan figure in a feature entitled "Goofy of the Apes," a send-up of Hugh Hudson's 1984 film, *Greystoke: The Legend of Tarzan, Lord of the Apes*. As a traveling reporter, Clarabelle discovers the lost Lord Goofstoke; Mickey and Donald, her sidekicks/assistants, draw the unenviable task of trying to civilize this ignoble savage. The preliminary sketches don't look terribly promising; in some of the drawings, Goofy sports an unruly mop of red hair that makes him look like a cross between Woody Woodpecker and a lion, and the story follows the live-action film too closely to have more than very short-lived interest as a spoof.

MICKEY, DONALD, AND GOOFY

Some of the most memorable Disney cartoons featured the star trio of Mickey, Donald, and Goofy—*Clock Cleaners* (1937), *Lonesome Ghosts* (1937), and *Mickey's Trailer* (1938). Despite the popularity of these films, the characters rarely functioned as a real comedy team. In most successful cartoon teams, the characters are either pitted directly against each other (Bugs Bunny and Elmer Fudd, Tom and Jerry) or they work together against a common foe (Jerry and Tuffy, Heckle and Jeckle, Hubie and Bertie). Mickey, Donald, and Goofy performed more or less in isolation, with a minimum of interaction occurring among the characters, which made it difficult to create situations for them.

"Ditch Diggers," a short Ches Cobb developed in October 1941, illustrates the problem. Goofy and Donald are workers on a road construction crew under foreman Black Pete. As a surveyor, the Goof struggles with a balky transmit (a telescope mounted on a tripod) in a running gag that recalls his fight with the piano in *Moving Day* (1936). Donald enters singing "Heigh Ho" from *Snow White,* and gets a faceful of dirt when he walks too close to an unseen excavator. He also takes an unexpected ride when he carelessly strolls into a section of pipe as a crane is lifting it into place. Both sequences are well developed and offer plenty of comic possibilities—but there's nothing for the characters to do together if they meet.

The problem of devising distinctive-enough actions for each of the individual characters to perform seems to have stalled the production of

Goofy's suction-cup climbing shoes put him in a precarious situation in "Mountain Carvers." Artist: unknown; medium: pencil, blue pencil

"Mickey's Follies" in 1937. Disney wanted to expand the format of *Orphan's Benefit* into a revue film that would include acts performed by "Mickey, Minnie, Donald, Pluto, The Goof and his girl partner; Clarabelle Cow and her Cow Ballet; Clara Cluck and her Floradora Hen Sextette" as well as the Three Pigs, Max Hare, the Tortoise, and other characters from the "Silly Symphonies."

The only consensus for the entertainment seems to have been that Goofy would perform a comic dance routine. No one seems to have been able to devise an appropriate act for Mickey, although the suggestions included a snazzy tap dance with Minnie, a magic act, and emcee duties. Donald also posed something of a problem—one improbable drawing shows him in a curly blond wig, imitating Harpo Marx.

Aurelius "Auri" Battaglia contributed a hilarious colored pencil sketch of Clarabelle reclining on the gnomon of a sundial surrounded by a chorus of cows in hourglasses for "Dance of the Hours." In another drawing, scores of Clarabelle look-alikes spoof the "By a Waterfall" number from Busby Berkeley's *Footlight Parade*. Unfortunately, "Mickey's Follies" never progressed beyond these preliminary sketches, probably because of the unresolved story problems and the cost of animating so many characters.

"Mickey's Bakery" spent almost four years in development. The idea of Mickey baking an elaborate cake was first proposed in April 1936; by January 1940, the story had been revised to feature Mickey, Donald, and Goofy trying to complete the biggest cake ever made for Mrs. Vandersnoot's society reception. Various gag ideas were devised, including whipped-cream fights, characters slipping on rolling pins, and a berserk machine spewing doughnuts all over the shop. One series of drawings shows Donald bending over and Goofy mistaking his upturned fanny for the top of

Goofy would have made a less-than-fetching harem dancer in "The Legionaires." Artist: Ferdinand Horvath; medium: pencil, colored pencil.

Rough designs for a bulldog admiral—presumably Mickey Mouse's commanding officer in "Navy Mickey." Artist: unknown; medium: pencil, colored pencil.

a cake—which he proceeds to adorn with pink and blue frosting hearts and the words "I love you." But the jokes don't add up to a story that could hold an audience's interest for seven minutes.

"Sunken Treasure," another uncompleted Mickey-Donald-Goofy short developed at the same time as "Mickey's Bakery," reveals just how many variations on a single theme the artists might consider. When the idea was first suggested in June 1936, the film focused on an adorable little kid who dreamed of an underwater adventure that included merchildren, King Neptune, pirate skeletons, and treasure. Two additional ideas for underwater fantasies were presented in April 1937: In "Davey Jones' Locker," Mickey went after the treasure and battled the octopi, mermen, and dancing pirate skeletons; Mickey and Donald pursued an exotic new occupation in "Pearl Divers."

Two months later, another story was proposed under the title "Sargasso Sea," with Mickey visiting either a floating island or Atlantis. A rough synopsis dated June 22, 1938, suggests turning Jules Verne's *20,000 Leagues Under the Sea* into a dream adventure for Mickey (although the author fails to mention just what Mickey would do aboard the *Nautilus*). In July 1938, Howard Swift suggested that Mickey and Donald become deep-sea divers in "Salvagers," while a memo from Jack Hannah dated January 29, 1940, reads, "Mickey and Pluto in diving costumes are hunting sunken treasure in the ocean—they are menaced by pirate ghosts trying to protect their loot."

The same folder also contains an undated rough storyboard for "Mickey's Treasure Hunt: A Deep Sea Story by Grim Natwick and Marc Davis" (who worked together on *Snow White* during the mid-thirties), in which Mickey, Donald, and Goofy salvage a treasure-laden shipwreck. "Mickey's Sunken Treasure," an undated presentation by Raymond Jacobs, ends with the trio stranded on

the archetypal desert island. Apparently none of these ideas pleased Disney enough to proceed to a full storyboard.

The most fully realized of the unproduced Mickey-Donald-Goofy shorts was "Mountain Carvers," a project director Frank Tashlin developed during the summer of 1939, which depicts the characters' efforts to complete a Mount Rushmore–like bust of a man with sweeping mustachios. The story opens with the front page of a newspaper that has the banner headline "Chiselers at Work on Hero's Head." While Mickey rides a jackhammer like a pogo stick, neatly cutting out the bust's lower eyelashes, Goofy ties plumber's helpers to the fronts of his shoes and climbs up the nose of the monument. In a complex

Clad in the garb of an eastern potentate, Goofy experiments with a hookah in "The Legionaires." Artist: unknown; medium: pencil, colored pencil.

Mickey, Donald, and Goofy try to hitch a ride from a passing mirage in "The Legionaires." Artist: Ferdinand Horvath; medium: pencil.

"Mickey and Claudius the Bee" would have taken a miniaturized version of Mickey Mouse into the world of the hive. The Queen Bee enjoys a bath in a lady's slipper-tub. Artist: Harry Reeves; medium: pencil; colored pencil.

sight gag, Goofy's pants fall down while he's on a ladder and a small avalanche fills them with debris; his struggles to retain his balance recall the precipitous sleep-walking scene in *Clock Cleaners*.

Donald, meanwhile, fights with a pesky little woodpecker who chisels some loose boards, Donald's lunch box, and part of the scaffolding into sawdust. As the comedy builds to a climax, all three characters fall off the bust, followed by a box of dynamite. The woodpecker pecks the box in midair, unleashing an explosion that blows the mountainside to smithereens. When the smoke clears, Mickey, Donald, and Goofy are perched atop the teetering remains of the scaffold; the woodpecker, caught between the plumber's helpers, flies off, using the handles as wings.

The complete storyboard for "Mountain Carvers" looks very funny, although the brash slapstick gags recall the cartoons Tashlin made at Warner Bros. rather than the gentler Disney shorts. Notes from a story meeting held on August 8, 1939, suggest that although he had some minor reservations, Disney was generally pleased with the film's progress. But he rejected a suggestion to add more characters, saying:

> I think it's more valuable to take a good situation and milk it. That is what you find Laurel and Hardy doing—the audience gets rolling with the situation … I think this is a gag-type picture that you shouldn't bother with story on or with too many complications. The audience isn't interested in that. We feel as we sit here that we have to have something to tie it together. But it isn't necessary … just enjoy each situation as it comes and not ask why.

"Mountain Carvers" progressed as far as a Leica reel (a film of the storyboard timed to a rough soundtrack), and Tashlin's notes indicate that a preliminary soundtrack was recorded. Photographs survive of a three-dimensional model of the mountain head, sculpted to aid in laying out the film and planning the camera movements. Nothing in the surviving records indicates why the film wasn't completed. (Curiously, none of the shorts Tashlin developed during his tenure at the Disney studio—January 1939 to March 1941—went into production, a fact that may have led to his resignation.)

Although the trio didn't appear in a feature together until *Fun and Fancy Free* (1947), numerous ideas for full-length films involving Mickey, Donald, and Goofy were considered over the years. Of these proposals, "Morgan's Ghost" had the most interesting history. Originally entitled "Pieces of Eight" or "Three Buccaneers," the typescript was submitted by Dick Creedon and Al Perkins in October 1939. Over the next two years, several artists, including Homer Brightman, Harry Reeves, and Roy Williams, reworked the idea as they prepared eight-hundred-odd storyboard drawings.

Mickey, Donald, and Goofy are cast as the proprietors of a modest tavern in the small New England village of Fish Haven. On a scary, stormy night, they're visited by Yellow Beak, a cranky parrot with a peg leg and a pirate's tricorn hat, who demands "a noggin o' sass" (sarsaparilla). He soon reveals that he's on the run from Black Pete because he possesses Henry Morgan's treasure map. Yellow Beak offers the others a share of the treasure if they will obtain a ship. But Pete overhears the plan, and, disguising himself as an old woman, he persuades the quartet to lease his ship, the *Sea Skunk*, and its crew of wharf rat seamen.

After a series of slapstick interludes at sea, Pete captures Yellow Beak and the map, and sets Mickey, Donald, and Goofy adrift on a tiny raft. Happily, they wash ashore on the very tropical island they've been seeking. The trio finds an old chest that contains not gold but the nutty ghosts of Henry Morgan and his crew. In a series of misadventures, Mickey, Donald, Goofy, and their ghostly allies rescue Yellow Beak and the map. The parrot confesses that a gap in the chart has to be placed over the tattoo on his chest to reveal the treasure's hiding place. After battling man-eating plants, quicksand, and geysers, they find the gold.

The artists prepared two endings for their saga. In one, Pete tries to take the loot but loses a game of Who's Got the Drop on Whom, and the good guys are victorious. In the more original alternate version, Pete makes off with the treasure, and Mickey, Donald, and Goofy return to their tavern. As Mickey laments their lost wealth, Donald bursts in with a newspaper: Pete has been arrested for passing counterfeit treasure! Yellow Beak announces that what they found was the decoy chest—the location of the *real* treasure is tattooed on his rump. The film ends as the trio pummels their erstwhile guide.

The tale might have ended there if Oscar Lebeck of Western Publishing hadn't been looking for a story for a Donald Duck four-color comic as a follow-up to "Mickey Mouse and the Phantom Blot," a comic book that had been published in 1941. He saw the material for "Morgan's Ghost" at the studio and liked it. Bob Karp, who worked in the Disney comic-strip department, reworked the script for Donald and his nephews; Carl Barks and Jack Hannah drew the panels. Although Hannah and Barks claim that they never saw the original storyboards, similarities in the artwork suggest they at least had photostats on hand.

The comic appeared in 1942 as "Donald Duck Finds Pirate Gold." (The title "Pirate Gold" had

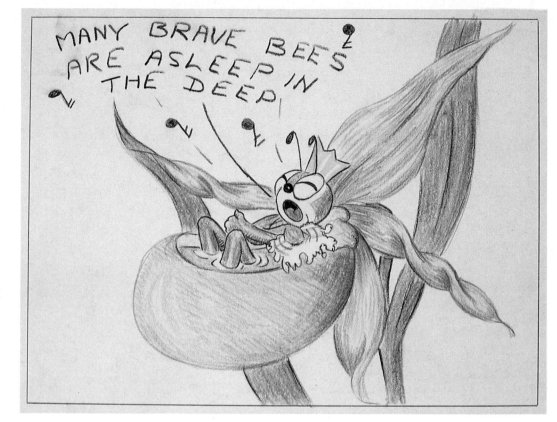

originally been used for a planned short involving Donald and an ersatz treasure owned by the aracuan, the zany redheaded bird in *The Three Caballeros.*) Hannah remained at the studio and directed many of the postwar Donald shorts; Barks went on to draw the Donald Duck features for the "Walt Disney's Comics and Stories" series. Original copies of "Donald Duck Finds Pirate Gold" are highly sought after by comic book collectors and Barks fans: a copy in mint condition may sell for $3,700 or more.

Fifty years after the fact, the preliminary artwork suggests that "Morgan's Ghost" might have been an entertaining film. Whether the artists could have found enough depth in the familiar characters to hold the audience's interest for over an hour, and whether the film would have enjoyed the same popularity as Barks's delightfully baroque comedy adventures for Donald, Huey, Dewey, Louie, and Uncle Scrooge, can only be speculated on.

III FAIRY TALES AND CHILDREN'S STORIES

Literary versions of old fairy tales are usually thin and briefly told. They must be expanded and embellished to meet the requirements of theater playing time, and the common enjoyment of all members of moviegoing families. The screen version must perceive and emphasize the basic moral intent and the values upon which every great persistent fairy tale is found. To these ends I have devoted my own best efforts and the talents of my organization, in full realization of our responsibility as a mass entertainer and especially our responsibility to our vast audience of children around the world.

—Walt Disney

ANIMATION IN GENERAL—and Disney animation in particular—has been associated with fairy tales since its inception. Commercial production of animated films began in America in 1913, when Raoul Barré opened the first professional studio in New York City. Two years later, Barré, Gregory LaCava, and Frank Moser launched their "Phables," one of the earliest cartoon series, which featured gnomes labeled "Joys" and "Glooms." When Walt Disney expanded the "Newman Laugh-O-Grams" from one-minute topical films to full-fledged cartoon shorts in 1922, he hoped to emulate the success of Paul Terry's *Aesop's Fables* ("sugarcoated pills of wisdom"), which had premiered the previous year. Disney based his new series on the fairy tales "Little Red Riding Hood," "The Four Musicians of Bremen," "Puss in Boots," "Jack and the Beanstalk," "Goldie Locks and the Three Bears," and "Cinderella."

Mel Shaw's realistic depiction of the cockfight in *Chanticleer* contrasts sharply with the Marc Davis–stylized rendition of the same scene (page 84). Medium: pastels.

A rough design for Goldie Locks in
"The Three Bears" shows typical poses
and expressions for the character.
Artist: unknown; medium: pencil,
colored pencil.

Opposite
Preliminary designs for
"Streubel Peter" suggest the
cartoon equivalent of a Dead End
Kid. Artist: Ferdinand Horvath;
medium: pencil, colored pencil.

Fairy tales offered a source of familiar stories that diverse audiences across America would easily recognize. Because the tales already existed in numerous well-known versions, the animators were free to adapt and embellish them; as long as they retained the basic plot, the artists could change details and add comic business at will. Disney later discovered that critics and viewers would object to any tampering with *Alice in Wonderland, Peter Pan,* and other stories taken from a single literary source. But as long as a little girl met a wolf and said he had big eyes, audiences would accept the film as *Little Red Riding Hood,* regardless of any modifications.

In an interview in *Wisdom* from 1959, Disney commented,

> From years of experience I have learned what could legitimately be added to increase the thrills and delights of a fairy tale without violating the moral and meaning of the original. Audiences have confirmed this unmistakably. We define the heroines and heroes more vividly; add minor characters to help carry the story line; virtually create such immortal friends of the heroine as the Seven Dwarfs. Storywise, we sharpen the decisive triumph of good over evil with our valiant knights—the issues which represent our moral ideals. We do it in a romantic fashion, easily comprehensible by children. In this respect, moving pictures are more potent than volumes of familiar words in books.

During the thirties, many of the musical fantasy cartoons in Disney's "Silly Symphonies" series were based on fairy tales, fables, or nursery rhymes, including *Mother Goose Melodies, The Spider and the Fly* (1931); *Old King Cole, Three Little Pigs, The Pied Piper* (1933); *Grasshopper and the Ants, The Wise Little Hen* (1934); *The Tortoise and the Hare, The Golden Touch* (1935); *The Country Cousin* (1936); and *Wynken, Blynken and Nod, Brave Little Tailor* (1938). Other "Silly

Symphonies" featured stories or characters reminiscent of traditional fairy tales—*Flowers and Trees* (1932), *Lullaby Land* (1933), *The Cookie Carnival, Music Land* (1935), and *Merbabies* (1938).

In these short films, the Disney artists began to explore the development of more fully realized animated personalities, an art they would raise to unprecedented heights in the subsequent features. *The Ugly Duckling* (1931, remade in color in 1939) represented one of the first attempts to generate real sympathy for the plight of a cartoon character. Previously, cartoons had centered on knockabout comic figures. Audiences might cheer when Mickey Mouse or Felix the Cat won a fight, but no one cared if either character got hit over the head with a mallet or spurned by a lady love. The characters obviously couldn't be hurt—physically or emotionally. But if the viewers didn't empathize with the awkward little cygnet, *The Ugly Duckling* wouldn't work as a story. Significantly, in the Disney version of the tale, the unlovely title character finds immediate acceptance when he's adopted by a family of swans; in the original Hans Christian Andersen story, the cygnet must wait a year to grow into his beauty.

Over the years, Disney remade—or considered remaking—many of the "Laugh-O-Gram" stories into longer, more polished films. He may have been especially fond of these stories or may just have regarded them as popular tales that offered interesting visual opportunities. Although he often recalled how much he had enjoyed the silent film of *Snow White* as a boy in Kansas City, he probably chose the story for his first feature for more pragmatic reasons, recognizing that it offered an appealing heroine, comic supporting characters well suited to animation, and plenty of dramatic action.

When he began planning *Snow White and the Seven Dwarfs* in the mid-thirties, Disney realized that a feature-length story would require more

BABY SCRUBS OUT EARS WITH - HIS SCARF -

SNOW BABIES

Walt Kelly's lively drawings of the elfin characters in "Snow Babies" have an unmistakable appeal. Medium: pencil, colored pencil.

Three 1938 sketches of Donald Duck as one of the tailors in "The Emperor's New Clothes" show the artist experimenting with poses and costumes. Artist: unknown; medium: pencil, colored pencil.

Opposite
Two years earlier, Ted Sears and Merrill de Maris had begun developing a more straightforward version of "The Emperor's New Clothes." Artist: unknown; medium: pastels, watercolor.

complex and sympathetic characters than anything previously attempted in animation. The heroines in *The Goddess of Spring* (1934), *The Cookie Carnival* (1935), and *Broken Toys* (1935) enabled the artists to hone the skills they would need to animate *Snow White*. Creating a realistic, feminine princess represented one of the many enormous artistic challenges the Disney animators learned to overcome, and the fairy-tale stories in the "Silly Symphonies" frequently provided them with a testing ground.

EARLY UNPRODUCED TALES

Development on "The Three Bears" began in 1936, and early in 1937, writer Homer Brightman declared in a memo, "We intend to make this a lively, tuneful Symphony, adhering to a simple story that will allow for funny, cute personality gags and situations." The artists prepared two sets of storyboards, one focusing on Goldie Locks [*sic*], the other on the Bears.

In both versions, Goldie is a chubby-cheeked moppet whose panties show under her short skirt when she bends over. She resembles both Little Red Riding Hood in the 1934 Disney short *The Big Bad Wolf* and Shirley Temple. (In late 1936, the artists considered using a caricature of the child star and hiring her to provide the character's voice but quickly dropped the idea.) There is an almost aggressive cuteness to the design that typifies late thirties cartoons and that seems excessive decades later.

The artists experimented with various looks for the bears, including teddy-bears-come-to-life and goggle-eyed versions before settling on a caricature of W. C. Fields for Papa Bear, dressed in big cuffs, a high collar, bow tie, and top hat. The idea of playing Papa as a pompous Major Hoople figure whose vanity could be punctured suggested numerous gag possibilities; neither Mama nor Baby Bear was developed to the same degree.

Shortly before the project was finally shelved in late 1937, Jack Rose and Dick Creedon came up with what they called "a shot in the dark"—having the stock Disney characters put on the story as a skit, with Donald as Goldilocks, Pegleg Pete as Papa Bear, Goofy as Mama Bear, and Mickey as Baby Bear. Apparently this improbable casting didn't appeal to Disney, and "The Three Bears" went no further.

Around the same time that they were developing "The Three Bears," the Disney artists were also considering "Streubel Peter" or "Slovenly Peter." The story of a rambunctious boy who torments farm animals only to have them take revenge in his dreams offered lots of potential sight gags. The preproduction crew clearly had fun drawing Peter painting the family cow and tying two pigs together so they flip over and over, etc., and had even more fun depicting the animals playing the same tricks on him. But, like many symbolic fairy-tale characters, Peter is thoroughly loathsome. A note stored among the drawings of his many misdeeds sums up the problem: "If we can't make Peter so violently bad that he is funny, the audience will think him merely a detestable character and won't like the picture. Possibly we might make him less hopeless and reform him in the end."

Water Babies, a 1935 "Silly Symphony" depicting the fairy-tale-like antics of a group of tiny boys who lived in a pond, had proved popular enough to warrant considering a sequel. In 1936, Walt Kelly, the future creator of "Pogo," made some charming sketches of minuscule children frolicking in a winter landscape for the projected short "Snow Babies." The wee tots emerge from between the scales of pinecones to ski, toboggan, slide down icicles, play Crack the Whip on the ice, and ride a miniature sleigh drawn by a field mouse. The minimal story would have centered on a cocky redhead and his interactions with the other characters. Kelly's affectionate preliminary sketches for "Snow Babies" foreshadow his drawings of Grundoon and the other child characters in "Pogo."

An enthusiastic memo from Dick Creedon ~~uly~~ 24, 1939, warns that the audience must ~~red~~ that the characters don't feel the cold, ~~esses~~ concern that the babies not seem lost ~~finity~~ of wild, rugged landscapes—icy ex-~~d~~ towering perspectives. Everything about ~~uld~~ seem *snug, intimate* and *gentle*." He

also suggests adding actions for the animals and small birds, noting that "their paternal, watchful attitudes will make the kids seem looked after."

(Disney did release a sequel to *Water Babies* in 1938, *Merbabies,* a plotless cartoon that is basically an undersea pageant for a troop of little girl mermaids. As he was under enormous pressure to complete *Snow White and the Seven Dwarfs* on schedule, he farmed the animation out to Hugh Harman and Rudy Ising, whose studio was short of work.)

In addition to these standard fairy tales and fairy-tale-like stories, the Disney staff researched poems and other material that offered visual possibilities. An undated folder of drawings reveals that they considered making a short film based on Lewis Carroll's nonsense classic, "Jabberwocky," prior to the *Alice in Wonderland* feature. The odd little pastel and gouache sketches include trees with faces, musical instrument/animal combinations, tree trunks that look like headless dancers, and a jub-jub bird made of bricks.

The rather surreal drawings suggest that the artists let their imaginations wander, but they scarcely reflect either the meaning or tone of the poem. "Jabberwocky" derives its appeal from the

curiously logical flow of bizarre words rather than from any concrete visual descriptions. Similar problems seem to have stymied an attempt to animate "Abdul Abulbul Amir," taken from Carl Sandburg's *The American Songbag*. The wordplays and tongue-twisting refrains are more fun than the story of the duel between the Russian and Turkish champions, and the artists don't seem to have found much inspiration in the lyrics.

HANS CHRISTIAN ANDERSEN

Walt Disney may well have felt a special kinship with Hans Christian Andersen. Both men were carried from poverty and obscurity to wealth and fame by their storytelling abilities. Both men had to overcome basically shy natures and learn to charm audiences. Both men created extraordinary bodies of work that continue to speak to children and adults alike. Andersen's fables provided Disney with the material for some of his most successful cartoons, including *The Ugly Duckling*, which Warner Bros. director Chuck Jones praises as "one of the best short subjects ever made." Not surprisingly, the Disney artists considered animating other Andersen stories.

In 1936, Ted Sears and Merrill de Maris began to develop a "Silly Symphony" based on "The Emperor's New Clothes" but abandoned the project, feeling that the ending was too weak. Two years later, a second crew began work on a version starring Mickey Mouse. Although it was listed in the studio files as a short, the number of sketches and the added plot complications suggest that the film could have been expanded into a featurette if not a full-length feature.

In the proposed film, Mickey, Donald, and Goofy are cast as poor but kindly tailors who share their meager resources with the birds and animals of the surrounding forest. When the Emperor comes to their shop demanding overdue...

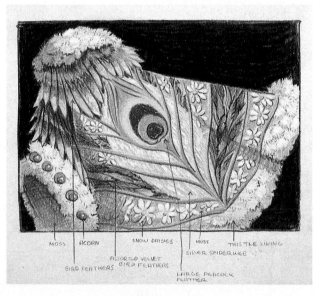

The elaborate robes of feathers and flowers made by the birds and animals for tailors in the Mickey-Donald-Goofy version of "The Emperor's New Clothes." Artist: unknown; medium: colored pencil.

Opposite
Aping the pose of Louis XIV in the famous Rigaud portrait, this Emperor looks vain enough to be duped by any unscrupulous tailor. Artist: unknown; medium: watercolor.

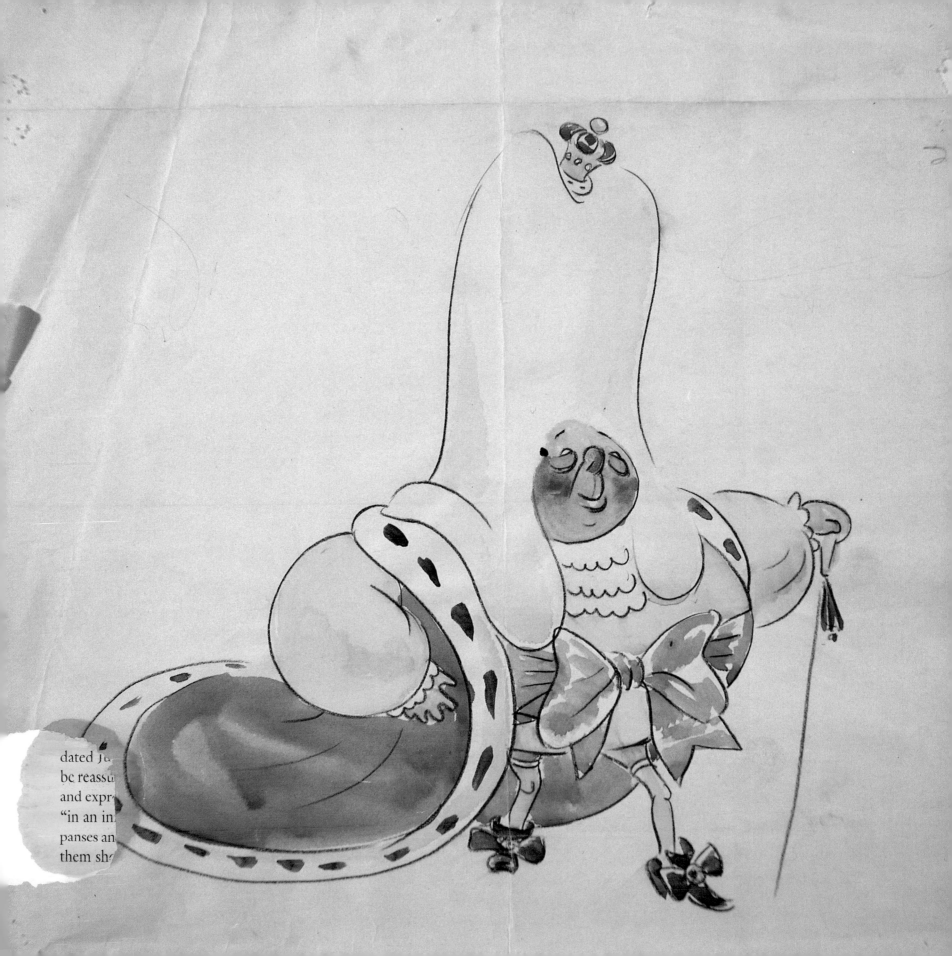

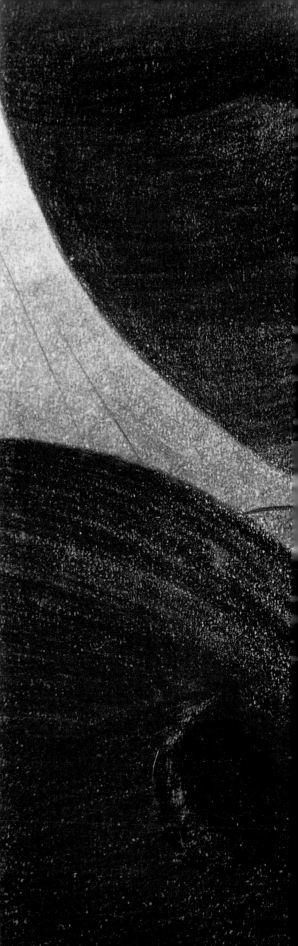

Kay Nielsen's preliminary drawings
for "The Little Mermaid" reflect
the wistful tone of the original story,
as well as the influence of the *Ballets
russes* designers. Medium: watercolor,
charcoal, pastels.

Donald and Goofy pretend to be sewing and weaving; Mickey explains that they're working with a special invisible fabric that can be seen only by those who are good and honest. The Emperor is intrigued by the imaginary cloth and insists that they make him a suit out of it.

Forced to go along with the hoax, the three heroes present the Emperor with an invisible suit that he dons for a procession. When a child declares that the Emperor is in his underwear, the Emperor chases the trio, cornering them in their shop. Just as Mickey, Donald, and Goofy are about to be executed, the birds and animals come to their rescue and present the Emperor with an exquisite robe made of feathers, flowers, etc. All ends happily.

Although the crew tried to devise enough business for the heroes to keep the audience entertained, they couldn't overcome the lack of sympathetic characters in the original tale. The Emperor is vain and foolish; the tailors who exploit his vanity are unscrupulous. Turning the story around and making the tailors into victims seems strained and unconvincing.

Another Andersen story that was repeatedly considered for animation was "The Emperor's Nightingale." An exquisite series of preliminary drawings made during the late thirties echoes Boucher's eighteenth-century chinoiserie wallpaper designs. The elegant Emperor and his court are masterfully captured in charcoal and pastels; watercolor storyboard drawings from the same era evoke blue-and-white Chinese porcelains.

In 1960, T. Hee, the codirector of the "Dance of the Hours" sequence of *Fantasia*, and future commercial animator Bob Kurtz began work on a stop-motion paper sculpture film of "The Emperor's Nightingale." The characters were made from layers of white-on-white textured paper and photographed on sheets of glass to suggest the limited perspective often seen in Asian graphic art.

"We wanted the light to ride on top of the sculptures and delineate them, but the different levels cast shadows on each other that ruined the silhouettes," explains Kurtz. "By using theatrical-style lighting and neutral-density filters, I was able to eliminate all the cast shadows and create a world of white floating on white. The characters moved, but they were defined by light pouring over their curved and scored edges. When we showed the test footage for 'Nightingale,' a live-action crew member who was at the screening said, 'It's real!' I've always remembered that—he meant that the figures moved in a way that suggested they had a life of their own." Kurtz regrets that he didn't keep any of the paper figures, as the carton containing the reels of test footage and the sculptures disappeared sometime after the project was suspended in 1961.

During the early eighties, preliminary work was done on yet another version of the story, with Mickey Mouse as the keeper of the real nightingale, for "Musicana," a proposed sequel to *Fantasia*. Although the Disney artists never completed "The Emperor's Nightingale," other artists saw the potential of this appealing story, including the great Czech animator Jiri Trnka, who produced a puppet feature based on the tale in 1948.

Several other Andersen stories went through various stages of development during the late thirties and early forties. "Through the Picture Frame," in which a little boy magically enters a painting in his family's parlor to rescue a princess, was extensively storyboarded. The snub-nosed figures of the boy and the princess are modeled after the precocious tots in William Steig's *New Yorker* cartoons. "Through the Picture Frame" seems like a natural story for an animated film, and it's unclear why it never went into production.

However, many of Andersen's most beloved tales have unhappy endings that posed seemingly insurmountable problems for the Disney artists. A Disney crew proposed concluding "The Little Fir Tree" when the title character achieves its am-

Opposite
The Emperor of China and his court examine the real and mechanical birds in this exquisite study for "The Emperor's Nightingale" sequence of the proposed Hans Christian Andersen feature. Artist: Ethel Kulsar; medium: pastels.

bition of becoming a Christmas tree. Andersen describes the tree being discarded and burned in a parable designed to warn children against wordly vanity.

Handsome pastel preproduction sketches were made for "The Steadfast Tin Soldier," but the ending, in which the title character melts in a furnace as his beloved paper ballerina catches fire, was deemed too sad for children. The great Danish illustrator Kay Nielsen did delicate gray watercolors that evoke the wistful melancholy of "The Little Mermaid," but Andersen's parable of Christian sacrifice also seemed too bleak to film. Decades later, John Musker and Ron Clements would transform this somber fable into an upbeat contemporary musical. After studying the early sketches, director Hendel Butoy decided to revive "The Steadfast Tin Soldier" for the continued version of *Fantasia* slated for release in 1997.

Many of these stories were developed as part of one of Disney's most ambitious projects—a combination live-action/animation biography of Hans Christian Andersen. Discussions for either a biographical film or a feature-length collection of Andersen stories began shortly before *Snow White* was released in late 1937. In the spring of 1938, Lady Mabel Dunn, the music critic for the *London Daily Telegraph,* visited the studio and suggested that Andersen's life offered a wealth of material. Discussions about the project continued off and on for more than a year while Disney personnel researched Andersen's life and work. Jean Hersholt's extensive collection of Anderseniana proved especially valuable, and in November 1943, Disney sent Hersholt a drawing from *Bambi* in gratitude.

Disney registered the titles "The Story of Hans Christian Andersen" and "Tales of Hans Christian Andersen" with the Hays Office in December 1939. Samuel Goldwyn, Inc., which had already registered "The Life of Hans Christian

Opposite
A more realistic style was used to indicate the live-action sequences in the biography of Hans Christian Andersen. Like Andersen, Walt Disney rose from poverty to wealth and fame because of his storytelling skills. Artist: unknown; medium: watercolor.

A coach races a train in the
Andersen biography. (c. 1942).
Artist: unknown; medium; pencil,
watercolor

Among the true events to be depicted in the biography of Hans Christian Andersen are the lonely author's return to his native Odense and his meeting with "the Swedish Nightingale," Jenny Lind. He kept a signed portrait of the opera star in his scrapbook. Andersen's inability to dance at a society ball may have inspired the story of "The Steadfast Tin Soldier." Artist: unknown; medium: watercolor.

Merton, a country boy who wanted to crash the movies in the same way that Andersen wanted to crash the theatre, was portrayed on stage and screen by Glenn Hunter. He was not only laughable and pitiful, but extremely sympathetic and loveable, and that is the way we feel Andersen should be—a likeable, sincere and interesting character throughout.

No final agreement had been signed with Goldwyn, and the deal was temporarily suspended, although Disney artists and writers continued to develop story ideas. Larry Clemmons submitted a draft entitled "The Story Teller" in December 1940, and a crew expanded the synopsis Perkins and Creedon had proposed the previous March. Work continued on the project despite the growing demands of war production. In April 1942, Disney apparently presented the preliminary storyboards to Goldwyn and some of his staff. In a letter dated May 1, 1942, William Hebert, Goldwyn's director of advertising and publicity, enthused:

> … the "preview" I had of this one, a few weeks ago, sticks in my mind as the most exciting film project I've had a glimpse of in some time. Mr. Goldwyn and I talked about it all the way back from your studio, and he was as het up about it as I was. I think that it would give both you and him great play for respective creative genius, and bring great credit on both of you, and I sincerely hope you won't drop it.

On September 17, 1943—nearly a year and a half later—an item in the *Hollywood Reporter* stated:

> Samuel Goldwyn and Walt Disney announced yesterday that the Disney organization will do an animated sequence for "Up in Arms." The sequence is already in work [*sic*] and will be presented as part of the climax of the film … They suspended work on their jointly produced feature "The Life of Hans Christian Andersen" at the outbreak of the war, so that Disney could devote more of his time to production of films

Andersen," asked Disney to withdraw the "Story" title, which he did. Despite the potential conflict with Goldwyn, work continued at the Disney studio on at least two scripts and preliminary artwork.

In March 1940, Walt Disney conceived the idea of a coproduction, with his studio animating the fairy tales and Goldwyn providing the live-action sequences. After a flurry of correspondence, Goldwyn sent over early drafts of three scripts that his writers had prepared. The Disney artists complained that Konrad Bercovici's *A Stranger at Home* failed to portray Andersen's life accurately, while the other two dealt extensively with Andersen's stay in a Copenhagen bordello.

In a memo to Walt dated March 15, 1940, Al Perkins and Dick Creedon presented their own account of Andersen's life, concluding:

> The character of Andersen we see as being somewhat similar to that of "Merton of the Movies."

identified with the war effort and international relations ... it is still on the Goldwyn-Disney agenda to be completed after the war.

The same day, Louella O. Parsons reported in her syndicated column:

Remembering the plans Disney and Goldwyn had to film the life of Hans Christian Andersen, I asked Sam what had happened. He said, "Walt has been so tied up with war films that the Andersen biography has been temporarily shelved." Personally, I hope it will be made soon. We could do with a few movies of that type.

(Disney did produce about eighty seconds of animation for the Danny Kaye musical comedy *Up in Arms* {1944}. The sequence was directed by Ub Iwerks and featured a group of characters identified as "Weavie-weavies." It is unclear whether the animation appeared in the final version of the movie. Contemporary reviews don't mention it, nor does it appear in extant prints; the artwork was destroyed after it was filmed.)

In 1952, twelve years after the discussions of a Disney-Goldwyn co-production began, RKO released the live-action musical biography *Hans Christian Andersen,* starring Danny Kaye. It was one of the last pictures Goldwyn produced personally, and film historians note that his commitment to the project led him to pay an inordinate amount of money to get the script he wanted. The consensus among the Disney artists was that "Walt let Goldwyn get it away from him."

CHANTICLEER AND REYNARD

Although Disney devoted considerable time, energy, and finances to the Andersen biography, even greater efforts were expended on what became the most fully developed unmade feature at his studio, a musical that would combine the stories of *Chanticleer* and the *Roman de Reynard. Chantecler,*

For Andersen's story "The Little Fir Tree" the artists tried transforming different types of trees into characters. Artist: Bill Peet; medium: pastels.

Edmond Rostand's 1910 symbolic play, focuses on a rooster who believes that his crowing makes the sun rise. Its satirical vision of a barnyard as a microcosm of society attracted large audiences in pre–World War I France. *The Romance,* or *Epic of Reynard,* a group of tales and poems first collected in Europe in the eleventh century, is one of the sources of the popular image of the fox as a sly trickster.

Initially, the two properties were developed separately. A memo from Ted Sears and Al Perkins dated November 27, 1937, questions the wisdom of buying the rights to *Chanticleer.* The piece was not well known in America and the story line would require extensive reworking. Perkins condemned the play as "highbrow"—a dire criticism at the Disney studio during the thirties.

Perkins also noted, "The experience with *Bambi* illustrates the difficulty of working entirely with animals, unrelieved by humans, and I think *Chanticleer* would possess many of the same problems. If we are going to use [*sic*] an all-animal picture, I think we should go the whole hog in a cartoon way, put pants on them and lean heavily on the comedy side, as could be done, say, in 'Reynard the Fox' or 'Penguin Island.'" (An extensive training program had been required to prepare the studio artists to draw the realistic animals in *Bambi.* The program added considerably to the cost of the film and necessitated pushing back its release date.)

Perkins likewise offered what would become the most common objection to the idea of animating *Chanticleer:* "The main problem would be to create a likable rooster in appearance and character that would draw the sympathy of the audience and keep them interested in his troubles and triumphs." Sears agreed: "We, or any other cartoon outfit, cannot depict a likable, interesting rooster character. Good animators have told

me this, and only some revolutionary change or inspiration would make a rooster character sympathetic."

"Reynard" was already in development in early 1937. In a meeting held on February 12, 1938, Walt Disney expressed concern that audiences might find this story "too highbrow" for a cartoon: "I see some swell possibilities in 'Reynard,' but is it smart to make it? We have such a terrific kid audience … parents and kids together … That's the trouble—too sophisticated. We'll take a nosedive doing it with animals."

He also expressed reservations about the personality of the title character: "Well, our main character is a crook, and there's nothing about him having the 'Robin Hood' angle. That was different because they built up these land barons and all that, but can you do this here? To begin with, it wouldn't be Reynard … He's not to be a murderer under any circumstances. He shouldn't take advantage of anybody but a stupid individual."

The Disney artists often made nasty characters into nice ones. In the original Collodi story, for example, Pinocchio is rude, destructive, and thoroughly unpleasant. As the men and women in the Reynard story meeting considered ways of making the devious fox seem sympathetic, Otto Englander remarked, "What appeals to me is that you can use Reynard's disguise in the service of good, rather than evil." Disney replied with unusual fervor:

> You'll have to do that or not touch it. Otherwise we will have people on our necks. The Hays Office is down on glorifying crooks because of churches and so on. They have a terrific influence. Even *Cock Robin* ran into things all over. We got letters from all over. A lot of people don't think that's the kind of thing we should do … trying to be too smart.

Early in 1941, the studio began to pursue the rights to Rostand's play in a package of

Opposite
"Chanticleer:" A study of the barnyard waking up anticipates the opening number from *Beauty and the Beast*. Artist: Marc Davis; medium: watercolor, pen and ink.

Above
One of Davis's preliminary studies of different types of chickens showcases his knowledge of animal anatomy. Pencil sketches of three subsidiary characters, and the Pheasant being made over under Reynard's supervision. Medium: pencil, watercolor, pen and ink.

A pencil sketch of a mole, one of the villainous Night Creatures from "Chanticleer," and the finished drawing. The title character encounters a new member of the farmyard community.

Opposite
Reynard attempts to woo a demure old hen. The elegant Pheasant, whose beauty dazzles Chanticleer. Davis feels his drawings for "Chanticleer" rank among the best work he did at the studio. Medium: pencil, pen and ink.

"French-controlled" works that included musical selections for the planned additions to *Fantasia* (Ravel's *Bolero* and *Danse Macabre* and *Carnival of the Animals* by Saint-Saëns) as well as Jean de Brunoff's first three Babar books. Disney offered $5,000 for *Chanticleer* in May 1941. Questions about the rights to the property were complicated by the discovery that Paramount owned a half-interest in the play. No one seemed to know whether or not that interest included motion picture rights.

Work slowed on "Chanticleer" and "Reynard" during the war, but story artists continued to study both properties and came up with the idea of combining them in 1945. One treatment from 1947 has Reynard leave an initialed handkerchief at the scene of his crimes—a device that prefigures the modus operandi of the Phantom in Blake Edwards's *The Pink Panther* by almost twenty years. Another draft suggests using Charles Boyer as a narrator.

The storyboards and treatments underwent numerous revisions during the next few years. The preliminary designs of a fox princess in a wimple, a crowned lion king, and rhinoceros guards in hooded liveries provided a jumping-off point for the artists

when they made *Robin Hood* twenty-five years later. Although the project was again shelved during the early fifties, the idea of a combined "Chanticleer"/"Reynard" was revived late in the decade and was slated to follow *101 Dalmatians*. On May 11, 1960, Ken Peterson sent Ken Anderson a synopsis of Disney's comments about the film:

> Most of his remarks seemed to be directed toward handling the story on the light side. He said, "Go for the fun stuff," and "We should really have a ball with this type of picture." ... Walt saw Reynard as a fast-talking manipulator who plays on people's bad traits and appeals to their gullibility. He is a swindler and a big promoter, but not too popular with his wife.

In a meeting held on August 24, 1960, Disney offered a more detailed opinion of how he wanted the film to develop:

> Basically, it's more or less a satirical thing on life: The Fox represents the conniving element, he's always misleading people... Chanticleer [*sic*] represents the solid citizen element... Chanticleer [*sic*] has got to tell the story. [But use] cute little characters, cute little shapes—those things could

The duel between Chanticleer and the Game Cock; one of the Night Creatures as a circus performer. The actions in the individual drawings are so clear, they already seem animated. Artist: Marc Davis; medium: watercolor, pen and ink.

come out of this thing, like the mice in *Cinderella*. ... Another thing to watch is that we don't get a little too sophisticated, a little too smart ...

Many of Disney's suggestions for the presentation of the song that would introduce Chanticleer to the audience anticipate the theatrical staging of "Belle," the opening number in *Beauty and the Beast:* "What we're doing here is a take-off of a musical comedy ... Have your chorus line and have people setting out tables. Open and they come in, then Chanticleer [enters]: Like you'd stage a musical comedy."

Despite his obvious enthusiasm for the material, Disney stressed the need to avoid the emphasis on aesthetics that had hurt *Sleeping Beauty* at the box office. He concluded with the problem that had haunted the "Chanticleer" project for nearly twenty-five years: how to make a sympathetic character out of a rooster.

> Get the personalities [into the minor characters]: that can't be an incidental thing, like the birds in *Sleeping Beauty* ... You have to get characters with sympathy, warmth, heart: You have to capture the imagination of the public ... When you use dogs, you don't need anything. But you take a rooster ... you don't feel like picking a rooster up and petting it.

A crew headed by Marc Davis and Ken Anderson spent months developing the story and preparing sheaves of preliminary art. Davis feels that his vivid preproduction sketches rank among his best work at the studio. Three decades later, a new generation of animators look to them as a source of inspiration.

"Marc designed some of the best-looking characters I've ever seen—those drawings want to be moved and used," says directing animator Andreas Deja, whose work includes the villainous Jafar in *Aladdin*. "Marc is not only one of the most skillful draftsmen the studio ever had, he's a fine artist in his own right. The designs for 'Chanti-

cleer' show the same level of graphic sophistication as his paintings. When that's combined with his very thorough knowledge of anatomy and the Disney appeal, the result is outstanding."

The early sixties were a time of transition at the studio, when Disney considered discontinuing animated features, which had become a small—and costly—part of his company's output. "Chanticleer" met an abrupt, unhappy end at a hastily called meeting.

"We had all the artwork up on the walls, and the money people at the studio came in like it was a funeral," recalls Davis. "We went all the way through the presentation and met with silence. Then a voice from the back of the room said, 'You can't make a personality out of a chicken!' They all filed out and that was the end of it."

The material lay dormant until 1981, when Mel Shaw presented a new treatment centering on "a magnificent rooster … the most MACHO in all of France. Like Maurice Chevalier, he was debonair, elegant, fearless, and most of all, protective of his many hens." This version of "Chanticleer" fared no better than its predecessors.

Any hopes that the Disney studio might revive the project yet again were dashed when the rival Don Bluth Studio's *Rock-a-Doodle* made its belated debut in 1992. This muddled adaptation turned Chanticleer into an Elvis Presleyesque rock and roll star. It opened to generally unfavorable reviews and quickly sank from view.

GRIMM TALES

At the same time that the later versions of "Chanticleer" were in development, studio artists explored the feature potential of two other familiar stories that had been made into "Laugh-O-Grams": "Hansel and Gretel" (which had also been used in the 1932 "Silly Symphony" *Babes in the Woods*) and "The Bremen Town Musicians." Work on "Hansel

and Gretel" began in the early 1950s. In 1961, Jack Cutting sent a series of memos to Disney noting that the rights to Engelbert Humperdinck's *Hansel and Gretel* could be purchased for about DM 65,000, but the idea of basing the film on the popular children's opera was quietly discarded.

A first-draft screenplay by A. J. Carothers dated September 27, 1967, eliminates the cruel stepmother and many other familiar elements. Much of the story focuses on the witch: She disguises herself as a beautiful woman to win the love of the children's father, which will somehow enable her to rule the world. She creates the gingerbread house to trap the children only after they interfere with her plan. Gretel doesn't rescue Hansel from a cage, nor does she push the witch into her own oven—the witch slips and falls in. (Instead of burning to death, she turns into a batch of gingerbread cookies.)

The sunny atmosphere of Chanticleer greeting the dawn (Artist: unknown; medium: watercolor) contrasts with the sinister attack of the Night Creatures. (Above) Artist: Mel Shaw; medium: pastels.

In Tyrolean costume, Mickey and Minnie
explore a garden of giant artichokes in
"Hansel and Gretel." Artist: unknown;
medium: pastels.

Richard M. and Robert B. Sherman, who wrote some of the most popular numbers in other Disney animated and live-action films, don't seem to have found much inspiration in the story. The songs they wrote for the film are saccharine and preachy. When Hansel and Gretel lose their way in the forest, a bunch of animals sing, "Chin up/ You'll be happy hearted/ Once you get it started/Up with your chinny chin chin!" A treacly ditty extolling the virtues of love runs through the film: "Love is the crowning glory/ There's no way to count its worth./But when you wear its golden crown,/ You're the richest man on earth!"

Sketches of Mickey and Minnie in Tyrolean costume indicate that the artists considered reworking the story as a vehicle for the familiar characters. The green-skinned witch they encounter looks more comic than frightening, although an elaborate chemical apparatus makes her cottage look like a mad scientist's eerie laboratory. It is not clear whether the Mickey "Hansel and Gretel" was begun before or after the Carothers script, but it never progressed beyond the early stages of development. (Disney often said that he wouldn't star Mickey in a feature because he felt audiences would tire of the character's falsetto voice.)

After Disney's death, a crew led by Ralph Wright worked on "The Bremen Town Musicians" between September 1968 and November 1970. A preliminary draft from October 16, 1968, begins: "Open on a screen full of psychedelic abstract forms that soon melt into a stylized map of Central Europe. The background music is rock and roll." The narrator explains that Central Europe has been the cradle of immortal music (Beethoven, Bach, Brahms, Mozart), then continues, "Some of our most modern music had its humble beginnings here, as authentically related in the Grimm Brothers tale of 'The Bremen Town Musicians.'"

In the original story, four aging animals who have outlived their usefulness—a donkey, a dog, a cat, and a rooster—decide to become musicians to escape being killed by their masters. After the quartet inadvertently scares off a gang of thieves with their caterwauling, they take over the thieves' hideout and live there happily. The Disney crew added a kindly human, Toby, a tinker with a tin ear (literally) who wants to marry Gretel, the Burgomaster's daughter. It is his idea to turn the animals into a "mod" band.

Toby rescues Gretel from the villain her father wants her to marry, "that awful Heinrick Stoneheart," with some help from the animals. He then fashions a tin ear for everyone in Bremen so that they can enjoy the quartet's rock concert—except Heinrick, who has to listen from the stocks with his natural hearing. The narrator concludes, "It took several hundred years for this music to catch on. You see, one has to have an *ear* for it."

The attempt to build a feature around such a lame spoof of popular music reveals how ossified thinking at the studio had become after Disney's death. In 1968, director George Dunning and designer Heinz Edelman had demonstrated the untapped potential of the contemporary animated feature by fusing the Beatles' music with wildly original visuals in *Yellow Submarine;* "The Bremen Town Musicians" seems decidedly old hat by comparison. Two decades would elapse before a new generation of Disney artists rediscovered the potential of animated fairy tales in *The Little Mermaid.*

Some of the whimsical little monsters the artists doodled while working on "Hansel and Gretel." Artist: unknown; medium: India ink.

IV WARTIME FILMS

We learned a great deal during the war years when we were making instruction and technological films in which abstract and obscure things had to be made plain and quickly and exactly applicable to the men in the military services. These explorations and efficiencies of our cartoon medium must not be unused in the entertainment field.
 —Walt Disney

WHEN AMERICA ENTERED World War II, movie stars and directors entertained troops, sold bonds, contributed to training films, and served in USO canteens; their counterparts in the animation industry applied themselves to war work with equal fervor. Scores of talented artists from Disney and the other Hollywood studios served in the Eighteenth Air Force Base Unit (First Motion Picture Unit) at "Fort Roach"—the old Hal Roach studio in Culver City. The animation unit produced training films under the command of Disney's old friend and associate, Major Rudy Ising.

Max Fleischer had pioneered the use of animated training films during World War I. Animation proved to be a more effective medium than live action for difficult and/or abstract subject matter: Studies conducted by the military indicated that their personnel learned material faster and with greater comprehension from animated films. But despite its large, talented staff, the Motion Picture Unit could not begin to meet the demand for training films for the burgeoning armed forces, and the Hollywood cartoon studios were commissioned to fill the gap.

Walt Disney may have anticipated the key role training films would play during the war. In early 1941, he produced his first educational short (at his own expense), a training film for Lockheed entitled *Four Methods of Flush Riveting*. The film, which featured limited animation of diagrams and schematics, proved so successful as a teaching tool that it earned the studio a commission from the Canadian government to produce an instructional film for a new antitank rifle *(Stop That Tank)* and four theatrical trailers urging Canadian citizens to buy war bonds.

Once America entered the war, the government demanded films at an unprecedented rate: By 1944, the navy alone kept an average of one thousand training films in production at all times. Prior to the war, the Disney studio's highest annual output had amounted to 37,000 feet of film—less than one-fifth of the 204,000 total for fiscal year 1942–43, 95 percent of which was commissioned by the U.S. military. (The figures seem doubly impressive when one considers that nearly one-third of the Disney staff had entered the armed forces.)

"We were in the war, and Walt was trying to do everything he could—he practically turned the

Goofy dreams of capturing Hitler single-handed in "How to Be a Commando." Artist: unknown; medium: charcoal pencil.

These images of a monstrous fly spreading contagion suggest that the Disney artists believed it was okay to scare an audience with "Public Enemy No. 1." Artist: unknown; medium: charcoal and pastels.

studio into a military base," recalls Marc Davis, one of the "nine old men" of Disney animation. "We all had to be thumbprinted and cleared by the FBI to work there."

Within hours of the bombing of Pearl Harbor, the U.S. Army commandeered the soundstage, parking garages, and other buildings at the Disney studio to store munitions and billet men for the defense of California. Identification badges were required for all studio personnel—even Walt and Roy—as some of the training films involved top-secret equipment.

These training films varied enormously in length, content, and style. "Although some of them were diagrammatic, many of them were fully animated," continues Davis. "We really animated these things, and we had some pretty handsome backgrounds. We used top-flight people when they were available. We did one series they called 'The Rules

"Army Psycho-Therapy" would have explored the physical and psychological bases of fear. Artist: unknown; medium: ink, pastels, gouache.

We made a lot of things for Lockheed. I made one that Elmer Plummer designed about using the torque wrench: Up until the time it was invented, you went by the way the wrench felt when you were tightening a bolt. But with aluminum parts, people were tightening them to the point that they'd crack with the first vibration. We'd work on these things in between other films—I'd dash out the animation in maybe a week. I don't know who the characters were; sometimes they were those dull-looking Mr. and Mrs.–type things.

The artists often had to explain highly technical subject matter in these films, and a cadre of scientists, physicians, military officers, and other experts oversaw their production. "They brought in authorities on many, many subjects, like the eradication of the anopheles mosquito, agriculture, making bread, et cetera," says Davis "They had professors coming out of the woodwork."

In a series of meetings held in August 1942 for "Public Enemy No. 1," an unproduced educational short planned for Latin American audiences about how flies spread disease, four doctors conferred with Ben Sharpsteen and his crew on the presentation of the information. The discussions ranged from how Latin American farmers butcher animals and the diseases spread by flies in the region to local designs for privies. A physician identified as "Dr. Ernst" declared: "I'm thoroughly in sympathy with scaring them with a dramatic presentation; we're going to be criticized for it; undoubtedly we'll face that, but if we don't have any grotesque scientific irregularities in presentation, we don't mind."

Sharpsteen summarized the studio's approach to instructional films when he observed, "The point I think most important to raise is that we are making the picture for Latin American people. Now what sort of language or picturization can we best use to reach them … best show them or convince them that they should get rid of the fly?"

of the Nautical Road'—thousands and thousands of feet that were done very simply on what various lights meant and so on.

"I also worked on some films on fighter tactics for the navy with Commander Thatch and the men who had won the Battle of the Coral Sea and the Battle of Midway. They had fighter tactics that were considered superior to everyone else's, so we made films to show other groups in the military how to use those tactics. I've been told by men who were pilots that they remember having seen the films, so I guess they must have had some impact."

"We did a lot of odd films," agrees Ward Kimball, another of the "nine old men." Pausing to consult the journal he kept at the studio, he notes an example, *The Right Spark Plug in the Right Place,* then adds:

ADRENAL GLANDS

A German spy attempts to inveigle a set of top-secret plans from Donald Duck in "Madame XX." Artist: unknown; medium: pencil, colored pencil, charcoal.

Goofy dreams of glory while performing KP duty in "How to Be a Commando." Artist: unknown; medium: charcoal, colored pencil.

Relatively little material from the training films—produced or unproduced—survives, as government agents took the cels, drawings, layouts, and preliminary artwork to ensure the security of classified material. The policy was even extended to cover the humorous "Private Snafu" cartoons various studios made for the *Army-Navy Screen* magazine.

The artwork that does remain suggests the diversity of these films. The singularly un-Disney-sounding "Prostitution and the War" used simple drawings and cut-paper figures that anticipated the minimal look of the United Productions of America studio's postwar cartoons. Commissioned by the Federal Security Agency, the film was based on a pamphlet by Philip Broughton that stressed the adverse impact of venereal disease on the war effort. After citing the figure of "seven million service days lost in WW I to VD," the narrator asks charcoal portraits of the Axis leaders, "Who fired that shot?" While Hitler replies, "Not this time—but I couldn't have done better mineself!" Hirohito answers, "Unfortunately, no, but it suits our imperial purpose."

A letter from Broughton dated June 13, 1942, stated that the film should be aimed at "organizations of all kinds—civic, church, college, defense councils, legislatures, auxiliary volunteer and professional groups." Broughton also noted, "We would want Mr. Disney's name on the title" and that "the job would have to be held to $20,000"—considerably less than one of the studio's theatrical shorts.

In contrast, dramatic pastel sketches on black paper were planned to illustrate the causes of fear for "Army Psycho-Therapy." Although no notes or script remain, the storyboard drawings and preliminary sketches indicate that the film focused on the action of the adrenal glands, the relationship between fear and stress, the importance of discipline and group identification, etc.

In addition to their work on the government films, the Disney artists volunteered for war-related services. Marc Davis and designers Mary Blair and Elmer Plummer painted a mural for the Hollywood Canteen; Davis and fellow animator Milt Kahl joined the group who painted a comic map of Hollywood on the wall of the nearby USO Center. The studio also produced approximately 1,400 logos for various military units and civilian organizations. Although it cost him about $25 to create each design, Disney refused to accept any payment, saying that he felt he owed it to the men and women serving their country who had grown up watching his cartoons. Donald Duck's volatile personality made him the most requested character for logos. He

Developed by Joe Grant and Dick Huemer, "The Square World" began as a satire on the rigid conformity of Nazi Germany—which would even extend to elephants. The two artists later expanded their idea into a possible feature. Medium: charcoal pencil.

appeared on more than three hundred of them, while Mickey Mouse was featured on only thirty-five.

WARTIME ENTERTAINMENT

As Ward Kimball notes, "Making fun of Hitler seemed to be an important thing," and many theatrical shorts produced during the forties satirized Axis leaders, military life, and wartime shortages, including *Donald Gets Drafted*, *The Army Mascot* (1942); *Private Pluto*, *Fall Out—Fall In*, *The Old Army Game* (1942); *How to Be a Sailor*, and *Commando Duck* (1944);. Nor was Disney the only studio to exploit war-related themes: When Disney's *Der Fuehrer's Face* won the Oscar for best cartoon short in 1944, the nominees included Tex Avery's *The Blitz Wolf* (MGM), *All Out for V* (Terrytoons), and George Pal's *Tulips Shall Grow*.

Mickey's nice guy persona didn't allow the artists to use him in violent situations or gags, but Donald's flash-pan temper and unfailing self-confidence could be played against all sorts of wartime misadventures. His roles ranged from the disgruntled Nazi factory worker in *Der Fuehrer's Face* to the eager, patriotic taxpayer in *The New Spirit* (1942).

The artists planned to continue Donald's comic exploits in the unmade short "Guerrilla Duck." Operating in occupied Malaya at "The Nippo Indo Rubber Company," he attempts to intercept a "Jap Troop Train." The story crew built much of the film around the visual gag of Donald bouncing off the elastic trunks of the rubber trees like a pinball ricocheting off bumpers. When he finally encounters the train, he gets his rump stuck in the mouth of a giant cannon in a typical piece of slapstick business. Some very detailed storyboard drawings were prepared for "Guerrilla Duck," but the artists don't seem to have been able to come up with an ending for it.

Although relatively few Disney cartoons contain ethnic stereotypes—far fewer than those of many other Hollywood studios—their depictions of Japanese characters in wartime cartoons often strike modern viewers as racist. While artists at all the studios drew unflattering caricatures of the individual European fascist leaders (Hitler, Göring, Goebbels, Mussolini), they uniformly caricatured the Japanese as a race with buckteeth, yellow skin, slanting eyes, and bottle-bottom spectacles. Donald's Japanese foe in the unproduced short

"The Lone Raider" is of the same regrettable ilk.

Slipping behind enemy lines in a (Chinese) coolie hat, Donald first identifies himself to the sentry as "Commando Duck"; catching himself, he replies in pidgin English, "Honorable fisheeman; so sorry please." Much of the film is devoted to Donald and the grinning little Japanese sentry trying to outwit each other. A protracted exchange of bows strains Donald's back; later, the sentry uses his feet to juggle the enraged duck.

The Disney artists considered two endings for "Lone Raider"; in one, Donald burns down the seaside industrial complex the sentry was guarding. The crew may have decided that the destruction of a factory wouldn't get many laughs, even from wartime audiences, so they developed an alternate finale that has the Duck trying to photograph the complex while fighting off a fractious crab.

Closer to home, the Disney artists planned to pit Donald against the wiles of a Garboesque enemy agent in "Madame XX." The storyboards begin with the camera tracking in on a single light in a window of the Capitol dome—a spoof of the opening of *Citizen Kane* (1941.) Inside, Donald is entrusted with a sheaf of secret plans and warned that spies would kill him to get them.

The deadly "seeducktress" lures Donald into her limousine with "Fall of Man" perfume, and eventually relieves him of the plans. During an ensuing chase in speedboats, Donald gets his leg tied to a floating mine, precipitating a series of near collisions. When he finally exhausts the spy, the Duck balks at taking back the papers, which the Madame's stuffed down the front of her dress; he kicks her in the behind and they pop out. He retrieves them and saves the day.

Goofy's maladroit enthusiasm also offered comic possibilities. Ralph Wright's story sketches for the unproduced short "How to Be a Commando" continue the popular "How To" series that began with the "How to Ride a Horse" sequence in *The Reluctant Dragon* (1941). While peeling potatoes on KP, Goofy dreams of becoming a commando and throttling Hitler. When Goofy arrives at the training center, the narrator explains the skills needed to crawl through enemy fire, handle high explosives, etc. Goofy tries to demonstrate these points, with predictably disastrous results.

A pretty WAC, obviously modeled after the girls drawn by animator Fred Moore, appears to

Goofy, a buck private, as his long-awaited romantic and professional opportunity in "Army Story." The artists don't seem to have been able to think of a payoff for the premise, and the preliminary drawings end in the middle of the story.

Wartime shortages and rationing provided gag material for all the Hollywood cartoon studios. At the end of Tex Avery's *What's Buzzin' Buzzard* (MGM, 1943), a cue card announces that in response to audience demand, another picture of an enormous T-bone steak will be presented; when the narrator of Bob Clampett's *Coal Black and De Sebben Dwarfs* (Warner Bros., 1943) declares the Wicked Queen "was as rich as she was mean," viewers see her lounging amid heaps of gold and jewels—and sacks of coffee and sugar.

The Disney artists planned to spoof rationing in "A House Divided," in which the Three Little Pigs would appear as defense-plant workers. Practical Pig rises early, bicycles to work, and buys defense bonds on his lunch hour. His idle brothers sleep late and are taken in by "Smitty"—the Big Bad Wolf recast as a black marketeer. The Wolf tricks the dim-witted Pigs into squandering their money on useless junk—earning them a lecture on wartime economics from Practical. Although Roy Williams's sketches look extremely rough, many of the gags are very funny. However, the Pigs' horror at being asked to pay *a dollar a gallon* for gasoline may be lost on modern audiences.

ENTERTAINMENT VERSUS PROPAGANDA

The line between entertainment and propaganda in animation grew extremely tenuous in the shorts *Reason and Emotion* (1943), in which fascism is presented as the triumph of irrational emotions over sanity, and *Education for Death* (1943), an adapta-

"The Melting Pot" would have used pidgin English and the graphic style of George Grosz to spoof German propaganda. Artist: unknown; medium: charcoal, pastels.

TEACHER

UND AMERICAN WOMEN! THEY ARE WORSE THAN THE
MEN! THEY DO NOT STAY HOME AND HAVE BABIES
LIKE OUR GOOD GERMAN WOMEN!

"Ajax the Stool Pigeon" (a.k.a. "Roland XIII") centered on a carrier pigeon whose fear of heights didn't prevent him from defeating a variety of Nazi spies, including a sinister bat, a glamorous pigeon, and a flock of vultures. His acrophobia did spoil the awards ceremony, however. Artist: unknown; medium: pencil, colored pencil.

tion of Gregor Ziemer's book on the indoctrination of children into Nazi ideology. Today, the approach to the material seems grimly heavy-handed. Not surprisingly, the same tone characterizes many unfinished wartime cartoons, especially one-shots involving new, unfamiliar characters.

In "Democracy," a film developed by Joe Grant and Dick Huemer, a little man named Jones and his family escape to America from Germany. As they call the other Joneses in the telephone book, they receive lessons in the freedoms guaranteed by the Constitution and the Bill of Rights. One American father assures the immigrants that they are protected from unreasonable search and seizure—unlike in Germany, where things are taken "for the Fuehrer's great army."

The surviving material suggests that the idea for "Democracy" never really jelled; the examples of the rights Americans enjoy have little to do with a long section depicting early Jones families facing tyrants, from ancient Egypt to the present. Another section chastises American citizens for balking at serving as air-raid wardens or contributing to scrap metal drives. A housewife complains that if they really need grease, "what good will my little pound

or two do every month at a nickel a pound ..." While each of the sections makes valid points, it remains unclear how they were supposed to relate to one another.

Huemer and Grant also collaborated on "Square World," which Grant recalls began as a satire on the rigid conformity imposed by the Nazi regime. Simply drawn pastel characters are shown being compressed into stiff, rectilinear shapes. However, the artists felt that the idea had the potential to be more than a propaganda short and tried to expand it into a feature. Had they succeeded, "Square World" would have represented a major stylistic innovation: The minimal figures suggest the semiabstract characters in the postwar UPA shorts rather than the lush visuals of the prewar Disney features. An adaptation of the story, in which a "Mighty-Highty-Tighty" ruler attempts to force his subjects to be as (literally) square as he is, appeared in the 1944 book *Walt Disney's Surprise Package,* along with preproduction art from other films.

The charcoal and pastel drawings for "Melting Pot," an unfinished short in a folder labeled "Dick H." (Dick Huemer), evoke the work of Weimar artist George Grosz. A Nazi lecturer de-

cries the evils of America in pidgin English: "Und we all know what happens when inferior races mix their blood! We get a land of democracy and gangsters! Und American women! They are worse than the men! They do not stay home and have babies like our good German women!" Apparently the film never advanced beyond the early stages of development.

The artists used a more conventional drawing style for an uncompleted short called "Ajax the Stool Pigeon" or "Roland XIII." The title character is a military carrier pigeon, the scion of a long line of pigeons who served in other wars. Unfortunately, Ajax/Roland suffers from acrophobia, which prevents him from continuing the family tradition. In addition to his neurosis, he has to battle a treacherous avian Mata Hari (who poses seductively on the hat of a lady spy) and the Nazi vultures and bats who work with her. The dramatic

Based on a story by Roald Dahl, "Gremlins" underwent extensive pre-production work in 1942–43. Gremlins lived peacefully in cloud-castles over Britain until the airplanes of the RAF "invaded" their realm, spreading destruction. The Gremlins swore revenge and began their career of sabotage. Artist: unknown; medium: pastels, watercolor, charcoal, red grease pencil.

sketches of airplanes, explosions, and searchlights piercing the night sky suggest that Ajax overcomes his fear, outwits the Axis spies, and carries a vital message to the Allied commander.

GREMLINS

The most ambitious (and thoroughly documented) of the uncompleted war films was a feature about gremlins. According to the *London Observer*, a gremlin was "an imp of bad luck to whom disasters are attributed in the roaring kingdom of the wartime sky." RAF aviators blamed them for otherwise inexplicable mechanical failures during the Battle of Britain.

Disney became interested in the project in July 1942, when he received an unpublished story entitled "Gremlin Lore" by Royal Air Force flight lieutenant Roald Dahl, the future novelist, children's author, and screenwriter. Later that year, gremlin stories began appearing in the American media. In September, both *Time* and *Newsweek* ran illustrated stories that stirred public interest in the elusive elves; a version of Dahl's original tale appeared in the British magazine *Cosmopolitan* in December.

But as public interest in gremlins burgeoned, Disney's lawyers discovered that neither the studio nor Dahl had exclusive rights to the characters. References to gremlins went back to the 1920s, if not earlier. Two other authors had already mentioned gremlins in books, and a third claimed the rights to them. These claims were settled when Disney promised to donate the profits from gremlin character merchandise to the RAF Benevolent Fund.

As more articles appeared in print with illustrations, and "gremlins" entered popular slang, other studios began to consider animating them. In early 1943, Roy Disney appealed to cartoon producers not to issue competing shorts, as the stu-

Often described as "elves of bad luck," Gremlins were blamed for a variety of wartime accidents. Artist: unknown; medium: charcoal, colored pencil, red grease pencil.

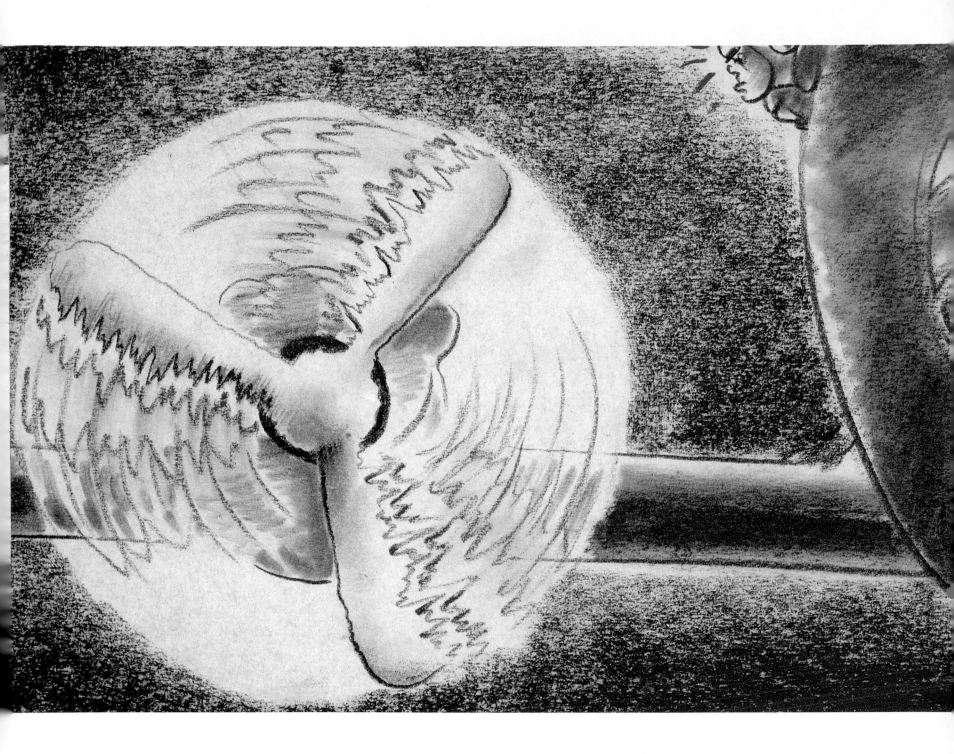

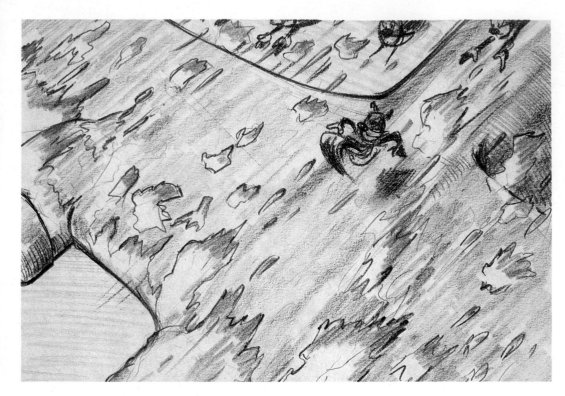

Making the Gremlins appear sympathetic and comic while performing acts of sabotage proved an insurmountable task. Artist: unknown; medium: charcoal, colored pencil.

dio had already invested $50,000 in the feature. All the producers complied, but Leon Schlesinger at Warner Bros. had two films that were too far into production to cancel. He took the word *gremlin* out of the titles, changing them to *Falling Hare* (1943) and *Russian Rhapsody* (1944). Director Bob Clampett wanted to call the latter film *Gremlins from the Kremlin,* after the song he had written for the homunculi.

The artists developing the gremlins project for Disney encountered as many problems as the bedeviled airmen. In Dahl's original tale, an RAF pilot sees a gremlin drill holes in his plane during a mission. After parachuting to safety, he gets acquainted with the diminutive saboteur and discovers that the gremlins are waging their own war against the Royal Air Force for turning their forest homes into airstrips. The pilot and his friends use a combination of aversion therapy (model planes that deliver shocks and splashes of oil) and bribery (gremlins like to eat used postage stamps) to convert the imps into "good gremlins."

But even after their conversions, the gremlins remain destructive and thoroughly unsympathetic. The rationale that they're avenging the ruin of their homes hardly seems to warrant their aiding the enemy—however unintentionally. The device of giving them a taste for used stamps seems contrived. (If they've lived in Britain for millennia, what did they eat before stamps were invented?) And Dahl needlessly complicates the story by adding Fifinellas (female gremlins), Flipperty-Gibbets (little girl gremlins), and Widgets (little boy gremlins).

Disney considered making the film as both a fully animated feature and a live-action/animation combination. The preliminary artwork is rendered in two distinct styles: dramatic studies of planes and pilots, which could represent either live-action or realistic animation, and cartoonier images of the gremlins. When the project began, no one knew exactly what a gremlin looked like, and although the artists experimented with a variety of designs for horned, bulbous-nosed little elves, no one seems to have had any clearer notion of their appearance when the project was finally shelved. (Dahl biographer Jeremy Treglown states that the author deliberately played on "Walt's anxieties about the exact appearance of the gremlins.")

Disney must have realized that the film would lose its appeal once the war ended, which may have been a decisive factor in his decision to abandon it. Audience surveys conducted as early as the fall of 1942 indicated that the American public was tiring of war-themed movies. In February 1943, an Associated Press story declared "Gremlin Stuff Is Getting Tiresome."

Although the project remained in development, Disney told Dahl in July 1943 that he had given up on the idea of a feature but would pursue

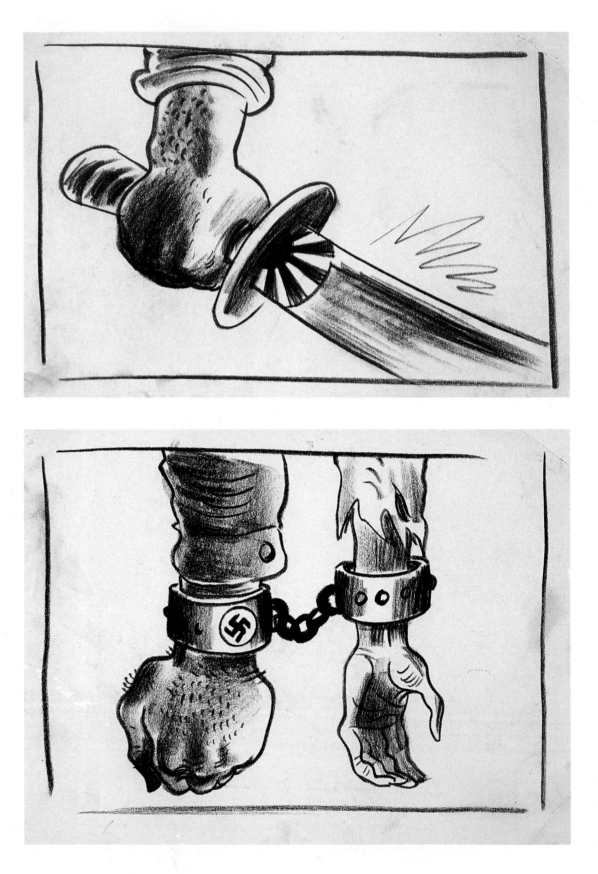

The simple charcoal drawings of hands for "Prelude to War" display quintessential images from World War II propaganda: a handcuff bearing a swastika, and a samurai sword embellished with the Rising Sun. Artist: Martin Provinson.

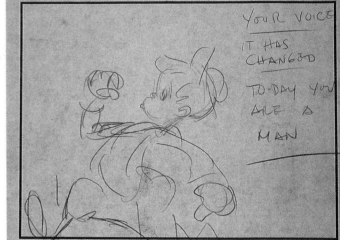

"The Laughing Gauchito" would have brought back the Little Gauchito character from *The Three Caballeros*. A vivid sketch suggests his mischievous nature; had his voice not changed, he would have taken his stage act on the road. A loose drawing reveals the diversity of styles in which the Disney artists worked. Not everyone appreciated the character's antics. Artist: unknown; medium: charcoal, pastel, watercolor, blue pencil.

CRACK!! CRACK!! CRACK!! CRACK!!

P-212 (R-1)

it as a short. In December, Disney wrote to Dahl conceding that the film was dead: "… We have given considerable thought to the possibility of making the *Gremlins* into a short, and I have personally endeavored to generate some interest among the various crews but haven't met with any degree of success. However, if we ever hit upon an angle that seems right for production, we'll get in touch with you."

Unlike the characters in most of the other unproduced films, Disney-designed gremlins did make a public debut of sorts. They appeared on at least twenty-eight military and civilian logos, and in 1943, a shortened version of Dahl's story was published, with illustrations from "the Walt Disney Production"—although that production never came into being.

SOUTH AMERICA

In addition to military training films and war-related entertainment, much of the Disney studio's production during the forties focused on Latin America. In 1941, John Hay Whitney, the head of the Motion Picture Division for Nelson Rockefeller, Coordinator of Inter-American Affairs (CIAA), asked Walt Disney to make a goodwill tour of Central and South America. CIAA officials, concerned that German and Italian immigrants there might foment support in the region for the Axis, felt that the popularity of the Disney characters would ensure the success of the proposed tour.

The offer could scarcely have come at a worse time. The studio was in the throes of the artists' strike, and Disney's debt to the Bank of America had reached $3.4 million. Whitney's offer to underwrite $70,000 in tour expenses and advance up to $50,000 for each of five films based on the tour may have convinced Disney to accept. In August 1941, he left for Rio de Janeiro with a group of sixteen, including his wife and several of the studio's top story men, designers, and animators.

New adventures for Donald Duck and José Carioca in "Carnival" included a visit to a sugar plantation, where they would have been caught in a "rain" of sugar, and a trip to the celebrations in Rio. Artists: T. Hee, Elmer Plummer; medium: pastels.

When he returned, Disney initially planned to make twelve short cartoons with Latin American themes. But during the summer of 1942, he decided to package the shorts in groups of four and release them as features. Richard Shale credits David O. Selznick with originating the plan, citing memos he sent to Disney and Whitney in January 1942.

Saludos Amigos, which opened in February 1943, consisted of the four shorts strung together with footage of the Disney tour: Goofy appeared in Argentine costume in "El Gaucho Goof"; Donald struggled with a balky llama in "Lake Titicaca"; José Carioca, the debonair parrot, made his debut in "Aquarela do Brasil (Watercolor of Brazil)," and "Pedro" depicted the adventures of a little mail plane in the Andes. Its enthusiastic reception in Latin America was dampened only by complaints from Cuba, Venezuela, and Uruguay at being "excluded." *Saludos Amigos* also opened to favorable reviews in the United States, although some critics expressed misgivings about its propaganda content. As Bosley Crowther of the *New York Times* commented, "... It certainly does well by South America—or, as the boys say, 'sells a bill of goods.'"

Saludos Amigos was eclipsed by the brighter and more energetic *Three Caballeros,* which opened on February 3, 1945. A technically sophisticated blend of live action and animation, *Caballeros* begins with a section about "strange birds": Pablo, a penguin who leaves the frigid Antarctic for the tropical Galápagos Islands; the zany aracuan, who pops all over the screen, and a little "gauchito" (a young Argentine cowboy) and his flying burro. In the second part of the film, Donald and José Carioca visit Baia in Brazil, then tour parts of Mexico with Panchito, a Mexican cowboy rooster.

The brilliantly colored, surreal action in the film troubled some reviewers: *New Yorker* critic Wolcott Gibbs noted that the "Jesusita" sequence,

a live-action/animation combination featuring Carmen Molina, Donald Duck, and a chorus of decidedly phallic saguaro cacti "would probably be considered suggestive in a less innocent medium."

The Disney artists did preproduction work on about ten other South American films or sequences, probably with another feature in mind. It's sometimes difficult to tell where one cartoon ends and another begins, as similarities in the artwork suggest that several of the sections were intended to segue into one another, as they do in *Three Caballeros.*

A musical sequence originally entitled "Brazilian Rhapsody" was completed and used in *Melody Time* (1948) as "Blame It on the Samba." In the finished version, a downcast Donald Duck and José Carioca (they're literally blue) appear at a café where the aracuan/bartender lifts their spirits with a samba cocktail. Ethel Smith appears within a giant cocktail glass, playing the organ as she performs the title song in a surreal blend of animation and live action.

The earlier sketches for the piece have the aracuan delivering pills shaped like the instruments mentioned in the song (*cabaca, pandeiro, cueca*) to Donald, José, and Panchito. After taking the pills (the aracuan steps on Panchito's foot to make him open his mouth), the trio begin to jiggle and metamorphose to the music. At one point, a chorus line of aracuans appears dressed as Carmen Mirandas, a gag the animators used in "Baia" with José. A similar live-action/animation mixture with Smith would follow this introduction.

An alternate opening for the sequence has Donald and José visiting a movie set to meet Carmen Miranda. In Carmen's dressing room, José sprays Donald with the star's perfume, which wafts them to Rio for the St. John's Day festivities. After watching fire dancers and other street performers, the pair leave to see Ethel Smith.

During a visit to a sugar plantation in Brazil, Donald, José, and a potbellied palm tree are buried in a rain of sugar. Artist: T. Hee, Elmer plummer; medium: pastel.

A surreal line of huge piano keys standing on end and turning into buildings appears in many of the "Brazilian Rhapsody" sketches. Similar images recur in other proposed South American sequences, which suggests that the artists planned to use them in transitional scenes.

Written by Homer Brightman, "The Laughing Gauchito" was planned as a sequel to "The Flying Gauchito" from *Three Caballeros*. (The winged burro even puts in a cameo appearance.) The little cowboy develops a laugh that can shatter glass and uses his new ability in a vaudeville-type act. He's a success until his voice changes: The shift to a lower register robs his laughter of its power—and ends his performing career. Frank Thomas did a good deal of animation on this short before it was canceled; the rough drawings display a charming élan.

Sketches for a short or sequence entitled "San Blas Boy" depict a little boy named Chico and his dog, Kiki, who live on the peninsula of San Blas in Panama. When they go fishing on the far side of the cape, they get caught in a storm that blows them across the isthmus; they have to be towed home through the Panama Canal. The loose ink-brush and color sketches suggest a combination of elements from "Pedro," "Pablo the Penguin," and "Laughing Gauchito." Notes stored with the artwork indicate that the film was in development from April through June 1946.

In contrast, no characters appear in the preliminary artwork for "Granada—Cape Dance," just castanets and a brilliant red cloak. The brightly colored drawings on black paper indicate that the three objects would perform a stylized dance. It's not clear whether "Cape Dance" was planned as an independent sequence or as an insert in a longer section, perhaps one involving a matador. The title indicates that the piece was set in Granada, a city in central Nicaragua.

THE FURTHER ADVENTURES OF DONALD AND JOSÉ

The bulk of the unproduced South American material depicts the continuing exploits of Donald and José Carioca. The bright colors, imaginative designs, and bold movements in these sketches suggest that the third Latin American feature would have exhibited the same rambunctious energy as *The Three Caballeros*.

As Cuba was a popular vacation spot for Americans (and because of the complaints about Cuba's "exclusion" from the earlier features), it's not surprising that the Disney crew planned to send Donald and José to the island. Detailed artwork of musical instruments and big-bellied palm trees reveals the preliminary research the artists did. Like the sections of *Saludos Amigos* set in Mexico, the Cuban material varies widely in tone. Delicate drawings by Mary Blair of little girl and boy dolls made from tobacco leaves contrast sharply with vivid sketches of cockfights, carnival celebrations, and José dancing with a line of cigars.

Donald and José befriend a plantation owner/bird (his wide hat, white suit, and pointed beak make him look a bit like one of the crows in *Dumbo*), who takes them on a tour of Cuba. They watch cigars roll themselves out of tobacco leaves—and smoke themselves into gray ash. One comic sequence is built around Donald lecherously pursuing a palm tree whose swaying form suggests the silhouette of a dancing woman in a feathered costume. When he finally catches the seductive figure, "she" turns out to be José with a few fronds stuck in his hat. Later, the faces of Donald and José fill the screen, then shatter into jigsaw puzzle pieces and tumble out of the frame in a bizarre but imaginative segue.

In the first of several Brazilian sequences,

"Lady with the Red Pompoms," José, Donald, and a toucan are smitten with Aurora, a pretty parrot with large hoop earrings. When she appears at a fountain as a washerwoman, all three characters attempt to woo her, only to have their efforts derailed by the aracuan. The artists apparently decided to drop both the toucan and the aracuan (who was becoming obnoxious) and add Aurora to the cast: She appears in three other segments, "Carnival," "Carnival Carioca," and "Caxanga."

For "Carnival," Elmer Plummer and T. Hee prepared striking color sketches of masks, costumed figures carrying lanterns, confetti, streamers, and other elements of the celebration. A stylized train ride recalls the "Baia" sequence in *Caballeros*. After Donald and José cut cane on a plantation, they are buried beneath a mountain of sugar. But most of the sequence is devoted to the festivities, which the artists evoke through costumes, rainbows, cockfights, parades, etc.

The gala mood continues in the sketches labeled "Jackson" (Wilfred Jackson) for "Carnival Carioca." These watercolors show Aurora in a Carmen Miranda–style hat joining Donald and José Carioca on their way to the carnival, presumably in Rio. In "Caxanga," she teaches Donald and José to play a tabletop game with matchboxes to the title song. Frank Thomas, who visited Rio as a member of the Disney tour, recalls that the game involved partners alternately sliding the box back and forth and withholding it. "After drinking for a while, it got tricky to remember whether you were supposed to slide it over or keep it," he says with a chuckle. Thomas also notes that "Caxanga" and some of the other songs in both the produced and unproduced South American films (including "Aquarela do Brasil" in *Saludos Amigos* and "Os Quindins de Yaya" in *Three Caballeros*) were the winning entries in an annual music contest. The Disney artists had heard them during the tour and decided to use them.

The war years proved to be a time of transition at the Disney studio. Although the production of military training films was financially rewarding, Walt apparently didn't enjoy working on commission. Marc Davis feels "this period robbed Walt of the kind of personal creativity that he normally would have had." To illustrate his point, he recounts an incident that occurred in 1946:

> One thing I never learned fully, although I knew it very well, was that you never just said something about a subject to Walt, you *showed* him something. One morning, about six months after the war, I ran into Walt. At that time, there was talk of going to the moon, and Chesley Bonestell had done these great paintings of space for *Life*. So I said to Walt, "You ought to do a trip to the moon!"—and if we'd done it then, we'd have been so far ahead of everyone. Walt looked at me and said, "For Christ's sake, Marc, I never want to do another training film as long as I live!"

Davis concludes ruefully, "He was so sick of professors and authorities and high military officers running his operation, he assumed I meant an educational film—which wasn't what I meant at all."

V FANTASIA AND ITS SUCCESSORS

It is our intention to make a new version of Fantasia *every year. Its pattern is very flexible and fun to work with—not really a concert, not a vaudeville or a revue, but a grand mixture of comedy, fantasy, ballet, drama, impressionism, color, sound and epic fury.*
—Walt Disney

ALTHOUGH MUCH OF Walt Disney's career was predicated on innovation, *Fantasia* ranks as his boldest experiment. The uncertain reactions it elicited from critics and audiences alike reveal just how innovative it was. No one knew quite what to make of it, as no one had seen anything quite like it.

Like so many of Disney's ambitious projects, *Fantasia* began modestly. During the mid-thirties, Mickey Mouse began to fall in popularity behind Donald Duck, Goofy, and, in some polls, the rival Fleischer Studio's Popeye. In late 1936, Disney began planning a two-reel short based on Paul Dukas's *The Sorcerer's Apprentice* as a kind of comeback vehicle for Mickey.

A chance meeting between Walt Disney and Leopold Stokowski at Chasen's restaurant in Beverly Hills in the autumn of 1937 changed the plans for *The Sorcerer's Apprentice*—and the course of animation history. Both men were dining alone, and Disney invited Stokowski to join him. When Disney mentioned the Dukas film, Stokowski offered to conduct the music and waive any fee. He also suggested that they collaborate on "a fanta-zee-ah," a feature film illustrating various pieces of classical music.

Although Disney initially passed on the feature idea, as the production costs of *Sorcerer* approached $125,000, it became obvious that a short film could never recover that investment, and he began to reconsider Stokowski's suggestion. In February 1938, plans were begun for a film tentatively entitled "The Concert Feature." Stokowski's contract to conduct *The Sorcerer's Apprentice* for free had to be renegotiated to include a salary and a change in musicians. For the film, he would lead his Philadelphia Orchestra, considered the finest musical ensemble in the country, rather than the Hollywood musicians who had initially recorded the Dukas score.

Stokowski, Disney, and the development artists listened to dozens of pieces of music between 1938 and 1943. They discussed possible selections in frequent story meetings, adding or deleting them and reshuffling their order of appearance. Among the pieces considered were *Don Quixote* and "Till Eulenspiegel" by Richard Strauss; *The Firebird, Petrouchka,* and *Reynard* by Stravinsky; Kodály's *Háry János* suite; Prokofiev's *The Love for Three*

The horses of Wotan's shield-maidens break through the clouds in a inspirational sketch for "The Ride of the Valkyries." Artist: Kay Nielsen; medium: pastels.

Oranges; Berlioz's "Roman Carnival Overture"; "The Ride of the Valkyries" and the "Pilgrims' Chorus" of Wagner; the polka and fugue from Weinberger's *Schwanda the Bagpiper;* Mozart's *The Magic Flute;* Debussy's *La Mer;* Holst's *The Planets;* Saint-Saëns' *Danse Macabre;* and a set of variations on "Pop Goes the Weasel."

In a meeting held on September 14, 1938, the tentative program for "The Concert Feature" ran: (1) Overture; (2) *The Sorcerer's Apprentice;* (3) *The Nutcracker Suite;* (4) Bee, Mosquito, Butterfly or Mechanical Ballet; (5) *Night on Bald Mountain;* (6) *Ave Maria;* (7) *Cydalise et le Chevre-Pied (Cydalise and the Faun);* (8) Fugue; (9) Relief; (10) "Ride of the Valkyries"; (11) "Clair de Lune"; (12) Animal Ballet; (13) Relief; (14) *Rite of Spring.*

As the Disney artists debated the possibilities of various pieces, they considered ideas that in retrospect seem improbable and even startling. In the September 14 meeting, Disney and Stokowski enthusiastically discussed the possibility of spraying perfume into the theater during key sections of the music. Stokowski suggested night-blooming cercus for "Claire de Lune," jasmine for "The Waltz of the Flowers," incense for "Ave Maria," and gunpowder for *The Sorcerer's Apprentice.* ("A very exciting smell. I love it.") The idea was discarded when Disney pointed out the problem of clearing the scents out of the theaters between sequences.

All the Disney features underwent considerable alteration during development, but the diversity of musical styles and the lack of a conventional story line caused *Fantasia* to pass through an unusual number of transformations. Revisions of the visual styles and subject matter for the individual pieces continued even after the final selections for the film were made (Bach's Toccata and Fugue in D Minor, Tchaikovsky's *Nutcracker Suite,* Beethoven's Symphony no. 6 *{Pastoral},* Dukas's *The Sorcerer's Apprentice,* Ponchielli's *Dance of the Hours,* Stravinsky's *Rite of Spring,*

"Clair de Lune" would have been the first piece added to *Fantasia* if Walt Disney had been able to realize his ambitious plan to transform the feature into a "musical and film repertory company." Artist: Sylvia Holland; medium: pastel on black paper.

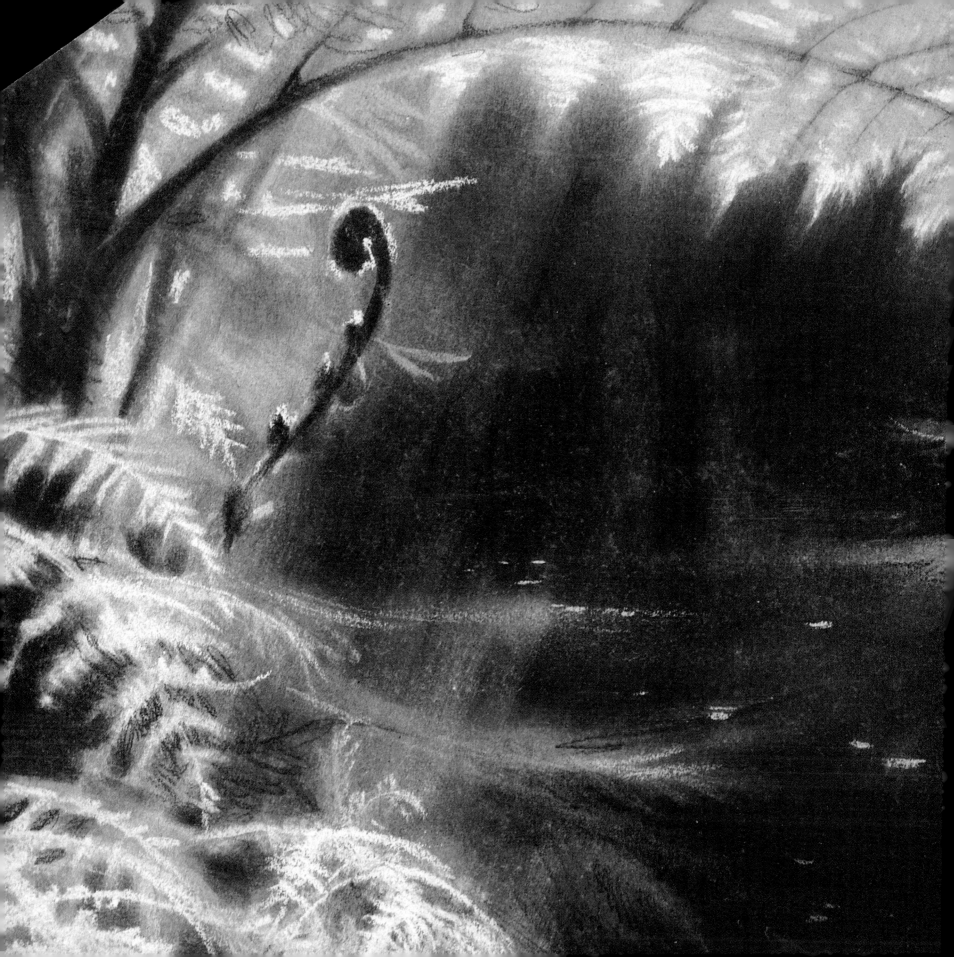

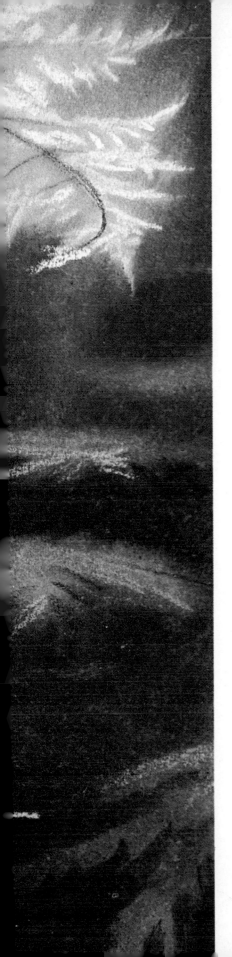

"Clair de Lune" would have combined evocative artwork of the Everglades with animation of a pair of egrets. Artist: Sylvia Holland; medium: pastel on black paper.

Mussorgsky's *Night on Bald Mountain,* and Schubert's "Ave Maria").

"The Pastoral Symphony" was originally envisioned as a languid, sensual evocation of classical mythology that would suggest the look of symbolist art. But when Disney liked an angular preliminary painting by Ken Anderson, the entire sequence was recast as an upbeat, Art Deco romp. Early sketches for "Ave Maria" followed the lines of pilgrims into a vast Gothic cathedral, ending with a vision of a stained-glass window depicting the Madonna, modeled after a Raphael painting. (Disney noted that this sequence could be deleted when the film was shown in non-Christian countries.)

As production continued and the film began to assume its final form, Disney seems to have realized just how big a gamble he was taking. Since the advent of sound film, music had played an important role in animation. In Europe, Oskar Fischinger and other early experimental animators had combined classical music and abstract visuals to produce films that suggested nonobjective paintings in motion. In America, a musical beat often supplied the rhythm of a character's movements, and the development and recapitulation of a musical theme offered a readily adaptable structure for a cartoon. Many of the best Mickey Mouse shorts, including *Steamboat Willie* and *The Band Concert,* had been built around musical motifs. The "Silly Symphonies" began with *The Skeleton Dance* (1929), a plotless fantasy set to Grieg's "March of the Dwarfs."

But *Fantasia* was more than an extended "Silly Symphony," as Disney knew. Shortly before the premiere of the film, he wrote, "No doubt, some unimaginative critics will predict that in *Fantasia,* the animated medium and my artists have reached their ultimate. The truth is to the contrary. *Fantasia* merely makes our other pictures look immature, and suggests for the first time what the future of the medium may well turn out to be."

Disney felt the limited motions and serene tone of "Clair de Lune" would offer viewers a respite from the brighter colors and faster pace of other *Fantasia* sequences. Artist: Sylvia Holland; medium: pastels, charcoal.

Despite the success of *Snow White and the Seven Dwarfs*, American audiences still equated animation with slapstick cartoon shorts. By linking his artists' work with great music and the talents of Leopold Stokowski, the Philadelphia Orchestra, and the eminent musicologist Deems Taylor, who served as the film's narrator, Disney was claiming a place for animation among the fine arts. Although he frequently dismissed the idea that the output of his studio could be considered art, Disney's reaction to a proposed gag for *Fantasia* in a meeting on December 8, 1938, expressed his grand vision for this film:

> We have worlds to conquer here … We've got an hour and forty-five minutes of picture and we're doing beautiful things with beautiful music. We're doing comic things, fantastic things, and it can't be all the same—it's an experimental thing, and I'm willing to experiment on it. We've got more in this medium than making people laugh—we love to make people laugh, but I think we can do both … Excuse me if I get a little riled up on this stuff, because it's a continual fight around this place to get away from slapping somebody on the fanny or having somebody swallow something … It's going to take time to get ourselves up to the point where we can really get some humor in our stuff, rather than just belly laughs; and get beauty in it, rather than just flashy postcards. It takes time to do that, but I think we will …

As the premiere of *Fantasia* neared, an extraordinary number of articles about the film appeared in both engineering journals and the popular press, most of them focusing on the originality of the idea of illustrating classical music and on the revolutionary Fantasound system, an important precursor of stereo. "It isn't that I deliberately set out to break movie traditions," Disney said in a *New York Times* interview shortly before the film opened. "But if someone didn't break loose with new things the movies wouldn't be where they are today. You'd still have 'Uncle Tom's Cabin.' Somebody's got to be a damned fool."

Disney had been called "a damned fool" for gambling on an innovative idea more than once (and would be again in the future). But he had something much further-reaching in mind for *Fantasia* than a single feature release. Although he had initially considered making "The Concert Feature" into a series, Disney seems to have conceived of his ultimate plan for a perpetually running, perpetually changing entertainment in a meeting held on May 14, 1940:

> You know, this is just a thought, but we might just take one number at a time—say, make one musical number a year. Then we can run it with the first "Concert Feature." We might run the first "Concert Feature" the second time, only this time we'll have, say, "Till Eulenspiegel," or "Clair de Lune," and we would keep adding to it and changing the program, just like the ballet does … [Audiences would] want to see their favorites again, and then we'd have one or two new numbers. It's something the ballet has always done. And I see a number I like listed, and I go back and see it again—it's never changed; the same scenery, the whole thing … I thought we wouldn't open with that ["Clair de Lune"], but later on, we'd put it in certain nights—we might even pass out the word that if there's enough applause at the end there will be an encore, and then if there's applause they'll run that.

"Walt was really reaching for the stars in those days," recalls Frank Thomas, one of Disney's "nine old men." "The success of *Snow White* really liberated him. He had struggled with the shorts because he could never get enough money to do what he wanted with them; he couldn't do everything he wanted to in *Snow White* either, but when it made so much money, it really boosted his morale. There was nothing he couldn't do!"

Fantasia premiered on November 13, 1940. Although it failed to score the critical and box-office success Disney had hoped for, he clung to the vision of a perennial *Fantasia* and continued to develop musical selections for the next three years. He foresaw a time when viewers would have to ask

The piebald faun and angry bee were designed for "The Flight of the Bumble Bee" from Rimsky-Korsakov's opera, *The Tale of Tsar Saltan*. Artist: M. Schwartzman; medium: pencil, watercolor.

SCENE 8 - BEE FLIES UP INTO FULL SCREEN

"not only where and when *Fantasia* is playing, but *what Fantasia* is playing."

An article in the *Hollywood Citizen-News* of January 20, 1941, reported that Disney was planning to make *Fantasia* into "something that travels around each season like the San Francisco Opera Co. or the Ballet Russe [*sic*]. The prospective patron will consult a program in advance, and determine his time of attendance at *Fantasia* on the basis of his preferences in musical numbers and motion picture characters. For *Fantasia* will vary from theater to theater and from week to week and from day to day. And it will become, if you please, a kind of musical and film repertory company."

The studio artists continued to explore the visual possibilities of various musical selections that could be added to Disney's "musical film and repertory company" for at least two years after the premiere of *Fantasia*.

"CLAIR DE LUNE"

Long before he envisioned using it as an encore piece, Disney had expressed an interest in developing Debussy's *Clair de Lune* for "The Concert Fea-

ture." The cool serenity of the music could provide the basis for an effective respite from the brighter colors and wilder actions that would appear in other segments. In a meeting on December 8, 1938, he explained:

> The audience likes to spend a little time in a show, and you can learn a lesson from this—it doesn't have to go at that rapid-fire bing-bing-bing tempo. And by getting something like this in, the rest of the "Concert Feature" seems shorter, because the audience has had a chance to rest, and they won't get worn out on the other stuff. It relaxes you—it's like getting a massage—and the five minutes just rolls by.

After viewing the delicate white-on-black sketches of water lilies, ferns, cypresses, and egrets the artists had prepared for the storyboard, Disney urged them to explore the effect of having the tree trunks and clouds suggest half-seen forms. "Just subtly suggest—just like in the moonlight you see all kinds of things, but you have to look twice. They've got to be cleverly worked in, not obvious."

The dimly perceived forms he suggested for "Clair de Lune" also offered an economic advantage: These images could be created by the back-

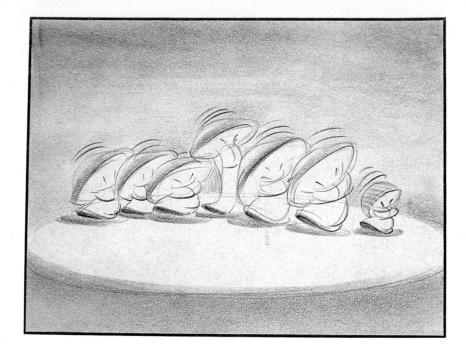

ground artists and effects animators. After *Snow White*, Disney's ambitious plan to release a new animated feature every year had taxed the studio's resources. "Clair de Lune" could be done for relatively little money.

The sequence was eventually animated and an introduction written for Deems Taylor: "No other composer has ever surpassed Claude Debussy in his power to create a mood and an atmosphere, particularly when he is expressing some aspect of nature. Here's a miniature tone painting of his that is a masterpiece of its kind. He called it 'Moonlight.'"

Although "Clair de Lune" was never released as a part of *Fantasia*, the visuals were reedited and set to "Blue Bayou" by Bobby Worth and Ray Gilbert in *Make Mine Music* (1946), the first of the studio's postwar musical package features.

"PETER PEGASUS"

Among the most popular characters introduced in *Fantasia* were the Chinese Mushrooms in the "Nutcracker" sequence and the rambunctious little black

Pegasus who cavorted through "The Pastoral Symphony." Disney hoped to bring them back in new animation set to Weber's *Invitation to the Dance* and/or Tchaikovsky's *Humoresque*.

Extensive discussions were held to create a story for the winged black foal the animators dubbed "Peter Pegasus." After sneaking out of his mother's nest, he might try to join a family of ducks, imitating their behavior like the cygnet in *The Ugly Duckling*. A series of misadventures was planned involving an angry bee he disturbed while inspecting a flower. At some point, he was to encounter the Mushrooms, who would do another dance—animated by Art Babbitt, who had drawn them for the "Nutcracker."

Animation of "Peter Pegasus" was begun, and the sequence was kept in production for several months as a "buffer" assignment for animators who ran short of work. The surviving drawings are not impressive: The character looks rough and cartoony and lacks the Art Deco grace of the creature in the original film. "The Mushroom Dance" never progressed beyond the storyboard stage.

Kay Nielsen's splendid preliminary studies for "The Ride of the Valkyries" evoke the drama of Wagner's music and the power of Norse mythology. Medium: charcoal, pastels.

NORDIC VISIONS

Richard Wagner's epic *The Ring of the Nibelungen* seems to have fascinated the Disney artists, probably because it was regarded as the pinnacle of operatic composition. (It doesn't seem to have been anyone's personal favorite; the story notes and memos suggest that very few of the people involved knew much about the music or the plot.) Over several years, various ways of adapting the music and/or story were considered and discarded.

A memo from Hal Thompson dated October 12, 1938, suggested using the "Forging Scene" and "Forest Murmurs" from "Siegfried" as excerpts. An undated note from an artist identified only as "John" urged Disney to add a sequence to *Fantasia* that would combine highlights from the *Ring* with an adaptation of a recently published children's book, J.R.R. Tolkien's *The Hobbit*. The tentative synopsis begins, "A Princess, descendant of the vanquished rulers of the City Under the Mountain, is living in genteel poverty in the land of the Hobbits. ... The Hobbit, shy younger son of the ruler of the country where the Princess's ancestors sought safety, loves the beautiful girl."

As late as February 24, 1941, researcher Bob Carr sent Disney an outline for a sequence that would combine "The Ride of the Valkyrie" [*sic*] with Kirsten Flagstad's performance of "Brynhilde's Song" (presumably her showcase arrangement of "Hojotoho" from Act III of *Die Walküre*).

After doing inspirational work for "Night on Bald Mountain," Kay Nielsen, the great Danish illustrator, prepared a preliminary storyboard for "The Ride of the Valkyries," working with story sketch artist Bill Wallett (who could imitate Nielsen's decorative style) and former background painter Sam Armstrong.

More than a hundred drawings were completed, most of them in moody shades of gray with

A noted set designer, muralist, and book illustrator, Nielsen infused his drawings for "Ride of the Valkyries" with a dramatic theatricality. Medium: charcoal, pastels.

Nielsen emphasized the contrast
between the earthbound human conflict
and the soaring spirits of the Norse
demi-goddesses in "Ride of the
Valkyries." Medium: charcoal, pastels.

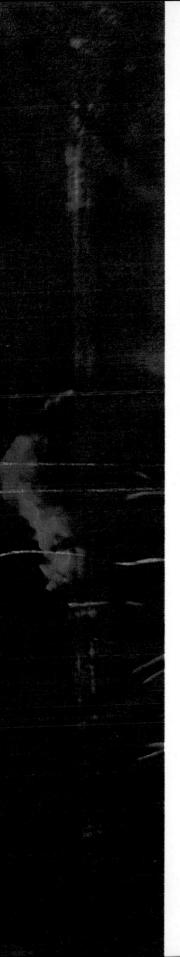

"The Swan of Tuonela" would have followed the journey of a Viking chieftain's soul to the underworld of Finnish legend. Artists: Sylvia Holland, Joe Stahley; medium: charcoal, pastels.

139

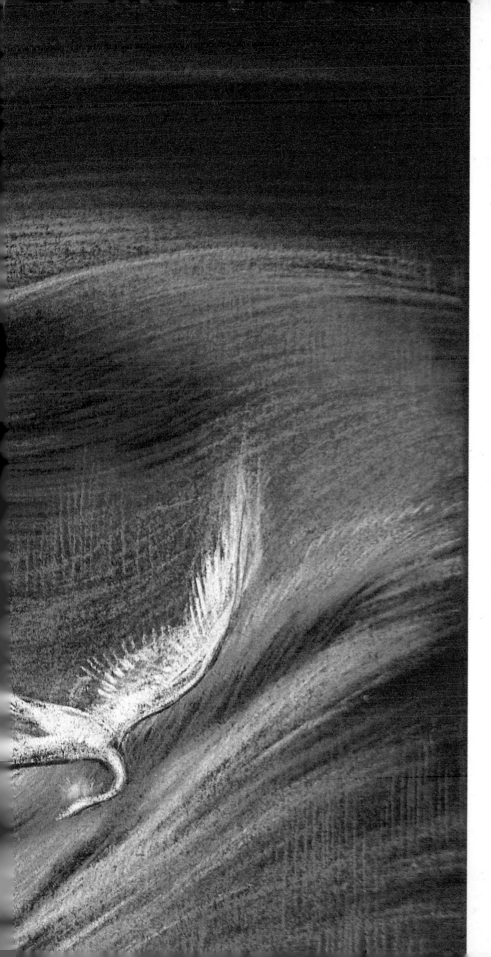

The Swan of the title guides
the boat bearing the Viking through
the treacherous currents of the black
river that surrounds Tuonela,
the mythical Land of the Dead.
Artists: Sylvia Holland, Joe Stahley;
medium: charcoal, pastels.

THE SWAN OF TUONELA

The title card and preliminary art for "Swan of Tuonela" depicts the mythical world of the "Kalevala" that inspired composer Jean Sibelius. The tone poem was initially conceived as a prologue to a never-completed opera, "Veenen luominen" ("The Building of the Boat.") Artists: Sylvia Holland, Joe Stahley; medium: charcoal, pastels.

angry red highlights. As two human armies meet in combat—a distantly seen fantasy of lances, shields, arrows, and battle horns—the nine Valkyries assemble on their Rock amid a gathering storm. The Daughters of Wotan ride their horses through the sky, galloping their steeds down vast banks of dark clouds that suggest gargantuan cliffs. The radiant figures guide the souls of heroes from the battle-field to a lofty Valhalla lit by the aurora borealis. In meetings, Disney had warned that any close shots of human characters singing would look silly on the screen, so Nielsen kept the figures small in an effort to preserve the heroic scale of Wagner's vision.

Despite Disney's admonition to avoid duplicating the look of "Bald Mountain," the artists suggested that the rising souls of the warriors could be created by shooting the reflection of a single mov-

ing piece of artwork in a curved tin mirror, a technique that been devised to show the dead rising from their graves in the Mussorgsky piece.

If the dramatic impact of Nielsen's drawings had been preserved, the finished sequence would have been stunning, but "The Ride of the Valkyries" was never completed. Although one possible factor was the identification of Wagner's music with the Nazi regime in Germany, Joe Grant recalls, "One of the reasons we kind of ducked it was there had been a lot of parodies of that 'Hojotoho' refrain, and we would have had to be very careful with it."

A great deal of preproduction work was also done on "The Swan of Tuonela." Although Sibelius's rather bleak tone poem might seem an unlikely candidate for animation, Sylvia Holland, Sam Armstrong, and Joe Stahley prepared a striking array of pastel drawings evoking a soul's journey to the underworld of Finnish legend. The mysterious swan of the title guides a Viking ship carrying a body through fire and whirlpools into a narrow cleft that leads to a luminous realm.

Although the drawings for it are more dramatic, "The Swan of Tuonela" probably would have resembled "Ave Maria" had it been completed: a stately series of long, slow tracking and panning shots with relatively little animation. In a meeting held on July 3, 1941, Disney told the artists that the images of the swan and the boat would be enough to hold the audience's attention if they were combined with animation of the water and a torch on the barge: "That would be all the action you need because you only need a little life to give you the feeling that it is alive—that it is not being slid along."

Like "Clair de Lune," much of "The Swan of Tuonela" would have been animated by the effects artists, and Disney hoped to get the sequence into production fairly quickly for "the effects boys to be working on as a cushion." Economic and other pressures intervened, and "The Swan" never progressed beyond the story-reel stage.

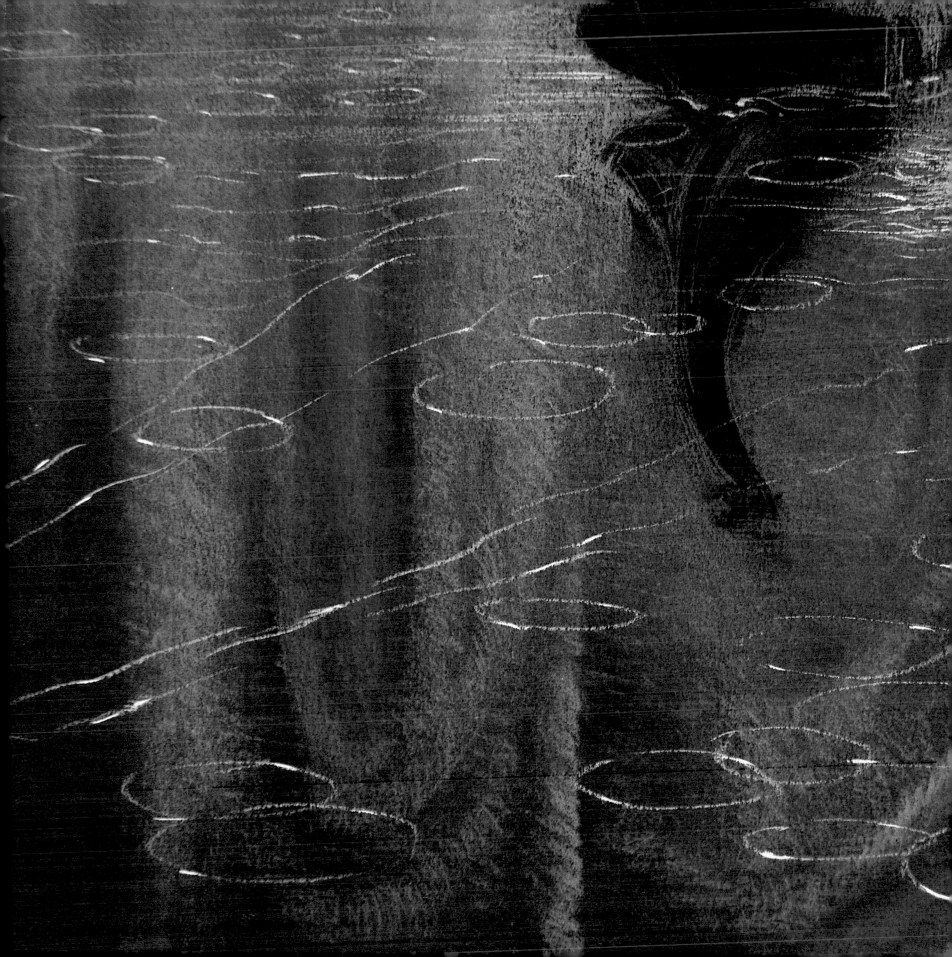

"INSECT BALLET"

Extensive plans were also made to combine several short pieces into an "Insect Ballet" sequence for *Fantasia*. "The Flight of the Bumblebee," Rimsky-Korsakov's popular showpiece from *The Tale of Tsar Saltan*, was an obvious choice. On September 14, 1938, Disney suggested having the bee appear to fly beyond the confines of the movie screen, using the highly directional Fantasound system to heighten the effect. Two years later, in a meeting devoted to the insect pieces, Sam Armstrong presented a storyboard that expanded on this idea. The bee would seem to dive into the audience: "You see a projected shadow of him on the screen … as if he were flying in front of the projector, and up and out again, and into the field, coming up and looking into the audiences' faces and flying off."

Set to a piano piece by Edvard Grieg, "Butterflies" was designed to capture the look of "a black enamel Japanese screen with the design embedded in the enamel," although the delicate preliminary drawings suggest lacquerwork rather than enamel. In this languorous fantasy of butterfly wings, flowers, and leaves (including, curiously, three cobra lilies—a type of insectivorous plant), the static "enamel" images would metamorphose into a realistically animated version of the same scene. Disney

In addition to "The Flight of the Bumble-bee," the "Insect Ballet" sequence of *Fantasia* would have involved diverse musical and visual styles. The comic "Mosquito Dance" would have been set to a piano piece by American composer Paul White; "Butterflies" by Edvard Grieg evoked the look of Asian lacquer-work; the insects in "Dragonflies" would have wooed to Chopin's "Minute Waltz." Artists: Sylvia Holland, Ethel Kulsar; medium: pastels.

liked the concept but insisted on the need for "an idea so that it is not just a series of pretty pictures."

Sylvia Holland prepared numerous pastel studies of a male dragonfly pursuing a redheaded female to accompany Chopin's "Minute" waltz. Their flirtation emphasized the visual patterns formed by the networks of veins in the insects' wings. Only a few preliminary drawings were made for "Mosquito Dance," set to the final section of American composer Paul White's *Five Miniatures for Piano*. Early drawings of a mischievous bloodsucker exploring a vulnerable human host recall Winsor McCay's *How a Mosquito Operates* (1912). It's unclear if the Disney artists were familiar with the earlier film, although many of them had seen McCay's *Gertie the Dinosaur* in 1914.

The idea for the insect ballet was eventually dropped, although a version of "The Flight of the Bumblebee" was used in *Melody Time* (1948), the last of the package features. In contrast to the realistic insect planned for *Fantasia*, the later bee was a broad cartoon character, and Rimsky-Korsakov's showcase for violin was rescored and set to a boogie-woogie beat. The idea of simulating the bee entering the theater was discarded, probably due to a combination of economic and artistic pressures.

The "Baby Ballet" was designed to appeal to what studio artist Bob Carr called "our country's great natural resources of bottomless Goo-appeal…" Artist: Mary Blair; medium: pastels.

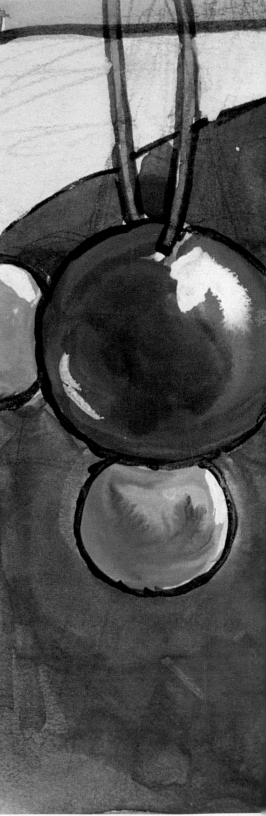

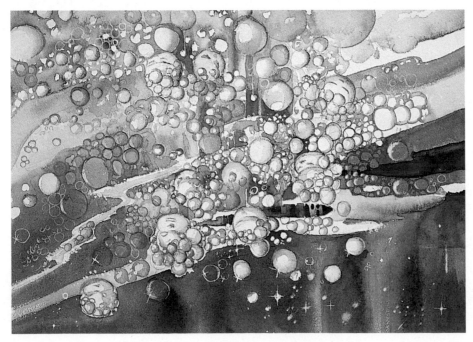

"Adventures in a Perambulator" would have depicted an infant's view of the world: a policeman reaches into the pram to tickle its occupant; two fantasies of bath time. Artist: unknown; medium: pencil, watercolor.

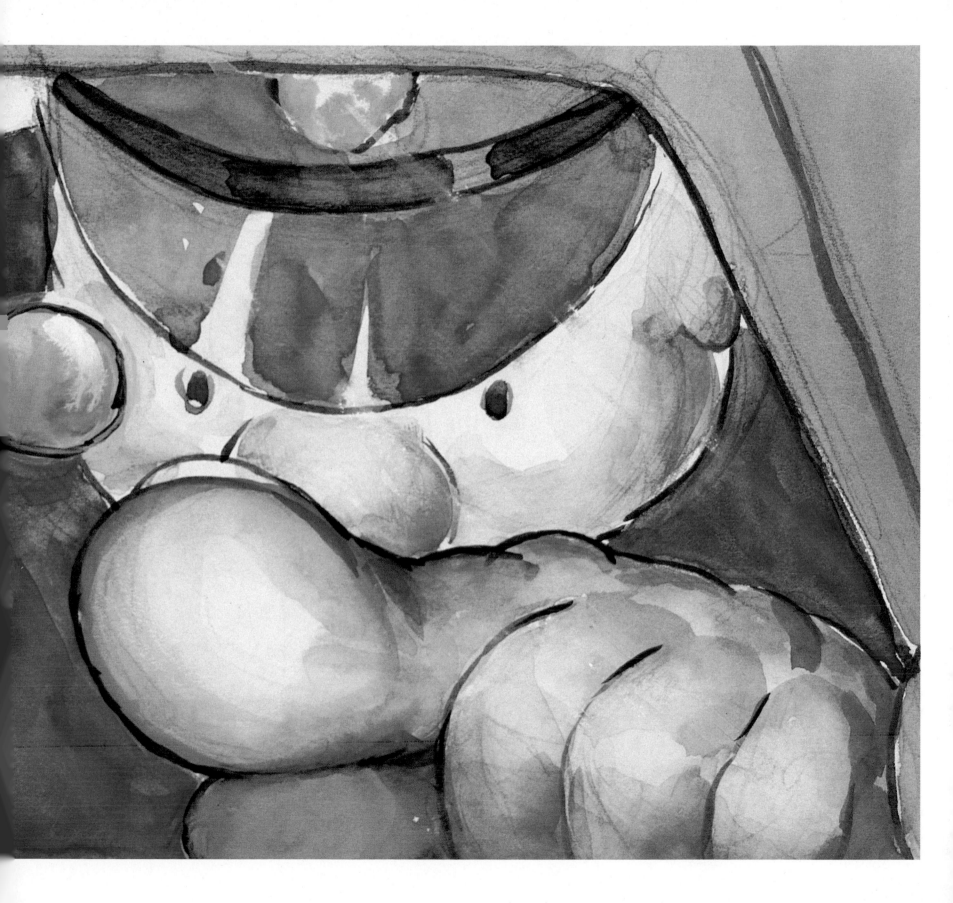

MISCELLANEOUS CONCEPTS

Cartoon babies had been the subject of several popular "Silly Symphonies," and the Disney artists developed two sequences for *Fantasia* involving animated infants. "Adventures in a Perambulator," keyed to a piano piece by the contemporary American composer John Alden Carpenter, juxtaposed the reality of a trip to a neighborhood park with an infant's rather fantastic vision of the world. A child's-eye view of a pack of friendly dogs drawn by Sylvia Holland shows an engagingly surreal collage of eyes, tongues, teeth, and fuzzy muzzles.

Preproduction work on the "Baby Ballet" stretched over several years before the idea was finally abandoned. In a memo dated July 9, 1943, Bob Carr noted enthusiastically, "Our country's great natural resources of bottomless Goo-Appeal have never been properly exploited. If audiences gurgle with glee at even a glimpse of a baby in a live-action picture, what would they do over a whole ballet of super-babies?" The sequence was originally planned for Chopin's "Berceuse," op. 57, but Carr suggested using a medley "of those stately yet tinkly, slow and simple little pieces that Handel, Mozart and Brahms loved to write."

The preliminary sketches by Mary Blair for this sequence depict a pastel

Opposite
Developed during the early 1980s, "Musicana" would have blended folktales with music from around the world. Mickey Mouse as the owner of the real bird in "The Emperor's Nightingale."
Artist: John Lasseter; medium: charcoal, pastels.

Above
The plumed serpent and mask were to illustrate Meso-American lore.
Artist: Mel Shaw; medium: pastels.

Below
The many adventures of the rainbow soundtrack reveal the unlimited imagination of the Disney story crew. Artist: unknown

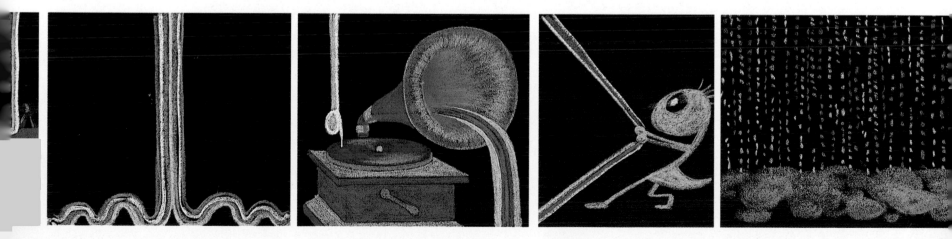

A haunting mask-like face drawn by Mel Shaw
would have appeared in the Latin American
segment of "Musicana." Medium: pastels.

world of infants with overly large heads who perform mock-balletic steps that recall "Dance of the Hours." A bathing scene supervised by a clutch of parental storks involves giant powder puffs and anthropomorphized diapers and safety pins. The visuals emphasize the bare bottoms of the tots, and the entire sequence exhibits a cloying, self-conscious preciousness that anticipates such saccharine licensed characters of the eighties as Strawberry Shortcake and the Care Bears.

The nebulous format of *Fantasia* allowed the artists to explore almost any idea during preproduction. At one point, they considered reworking some of the early black-and-white "Silly Symphonies" as color segments. Plans for a "Flower Ballet" called for "slightly humanized" plants reminiscent of the ones in *Flowers and Trees*. Disney also considered adding "brief live-action biographical sketches of various composers to be included in a future *Fantasia* to provide a contrast to animation," and preparations were begun for a sequence about Niccolò Paganini to accompany animation of his "Moto Perpetuo."

The artists also considered expanding the adventures of the semiabstract soundtrack character in "Soundtrack Impressions," which may have been planned as a short cartoon or a sequence for *Fantasia*. Although undated, the pastel-on-black-paper drawings appear to have been done during the war. A rainbow of sound flows out of the horn of an antique gramophone and is transformed by its environment. It gets whirled in a cocktail shaker, flattened on an anvil, scrambled by an eggbeater, and shredded in a meat grinder—actions that would obviously be cued to sound effects and musical changes. In some of the drawings, the fragments form American, British, and Soviet flags, semiabstract figures of dancers, and an odd little character based on an eighth note. The sequence doesn't seem to have progressed beyond these early sketches.

THE END OF AN ERA

The initially disappointing performance of *Fantasia* at the box office prevented Disney from realizing his vision of a constantly changing animated repertory piece. The film opened to mixed and even vitriolic reviews. American audiences balked at paying road-show prices, especially for children, to see an animated film. The war in Europe cut off important markets that had provided up to 40 percent of the studio's revenue. *Fantasia* had cost $2.28 million, about the same as *The Wizard of Oz*, which had been released the year before, but it failed to attract the large family audiences that had made *Snow White* such a huge success.

In addition to providing a regular source of revenue, preparing a revised edition of *Fantasia* every year would have enabled Disney to continue investigating new directions in the art of animation. Since 1928, he had reinvested most of his profits in an unparalleled program of research and experimentation. The "musical and film repertory company" he envisioned would have allowed him to continue to extend the boundaries of the medium, exploring color, motion, sound, and graphic styles as well as technological innovations.

The initially cool reception that greeted his masterpiece was a severe blow to Disney. Between the premieres of *Steamboat Willie* in 1928 and *Fantasia* in 1940, he had received little but acclaim. Almost every film had broken new ground, and he had eclipsed virtually every other artist and producer in the animation business. The failure of *Fantasia* marked the end of that era—and the beginning of Disney's disenchantment with animation.

"Although he never lost his enthusiasm for the film, the failure of *Fantasia* was extremely depressing to Walt," adds Joe Grant. "I remember on the way back from the New York premiere, he said something to the effect of 'All that work and all that fanfare ...' But, like every other time something went wrong, his basic attitude was 'Fine, that didn't work, what's the next project?' He realized that he had gone over the public's head with *Fantasia,* and that he had also disappointed them, because the film wasn't what they expected from Disney—he knew that when he put Mickey in 'The Sorcerer's Apprentice.' But you wouldn't find him grieving."

After the war, Disney artists did continue to explore the possibilities of blending music and animation in the so-called package features: *Make Mine Music* (1946), *Fun and Fancy Free* (1947), and *Melody Time* (1948). These films combined songs by popular performers—Dinah Shore, the Andrews Sisters, Roy Rogers, Dennis Day—and broad cartoon visuals. Both the music and the animation were considerably less ambitious than those in *Fantasia.* Although some of the individual sequences are amusing, these films lack the daring originality that made *Fantasia* a milestone in film history. All three failed to generate much interest at the box office, and Disney's vision of fusing music and animation into a revolutionary new art form was quietly abandoned.

"I think the failure of *Fantasia* hurt Walt, because it kept him from experimenting," says Frank Thomas. "There are some experimental things in the postwar 'package pictures,' but none of them were very well done. If any of those films had gone over, it would have picked him up. He had a lot of experimental ideas, but he didn't have the money to push any of them. When he tried to do one or two of them in the package pictures, they didn't go over."

The Disney artists agree that *Fantasia* was "about thirty years ahead of its time," a belief the film's subsequent success tends to confirm. The highly successful 1969 rerelease of *Fantasia* showed that teenagers and young adults were more receptive to Disney's great audiovisual experiment than the previous generation had been. The film became one of the great animated "head trip" movies of the era, rivaling *Yellow Submarine* and Ralph Bakshi's *Fritz the Cat*—an image its new psychedelic poster underscored. This belated commercial success led Disney and other studios to reconsider the possibilities of animated musical features.

During 1982–83, a crew at Disney began developing "Musicana," which inspirational artist Mel Shaw says would have combined "ethnic tales from around the world with the music of the various countries." Sibelius's *Finlandia* was chosen for a battle between an Ice God and a Sun Goddess that produced the myriad lakes of Scandinavia. Shaw's powerful pastel drawings show the half-seen figure of the Ice God emerging from cloud banks and craggy mountains. A sequence set in the Andes involving a beautiful bird/girl was intended to illustrate the songs of Yma Sumac. The United States would have been represented in a jazz fantasy on a Southern bayou featuring caricatures of Louis Armstrong and Ella Fitzgerald as frogs.

John Lasseter, who later won an Oscar for the computer-animated film *Tin Toy,* worked on a version of "The Emperor's Nightingale" with Mickey Mouse as the owner/caretaker of the real bird. Although the preliminary art contains some unusual touches, including Death appearing to the Emperor in the flamboyant makeup of a Peking opera performer, the designs lack the elegance of the version developed at the studio during the thirties. "Musicana" was eventually shelved in favor of *Mickey's Christmas Carol* (1983), a featurette adapted from Dickens's holiday classic.

After the fiftieth-anniversary celebrations in 1990, *Fantasia* was released on video in 1991 and sold a record-breaking 14.2 million units. (Four other Disney features, *Beauty and the Beast, Aladdin, Snow White,* and *The Lion King,* soon topped its record.) Walt Disney Pictures announced that future theatrical releases would include new animated sequences, although the musical selections and the nature of the visuals had yet to be determined. Asked why the studio would tamper with a film that had attained the status of a classic, Roy E. Disney replied:

Why not is probably a better question. It was one of those things that stuck in my mind for a long time because it was such a logical notion. One day *very* shortly after Michael and Frank {Chairman of the Board and Chief Executive Officer Michael Eisner and the late President and Chief Operating Officer Frank Wells} came into the company, Michael and I were having lunch, talking about animation. I mentioned the idea to him, and it was as if a big lightbulb went on over his head—he remembered it very clearly, too.

So when we decided we were going to go out on video with the picture, it seemed that the natural thing to do was simultaneously say, 'Okay, we're finally going to carry out that original dream and start to replenish the film.'

Eventually we'll wind up with two *Fantasia*s, but it will take about ten years—it's hard to guess exactly how long.

Walt Disney foresaw the enduring appeal of the film when he wrote in 1940, "*Fantasia* is timeless. It may run ten, twenty or thirty years. It may run after I'm gone. *Fantasia* is an idea in itself. I can never build another *Fantasia*. I can improve. I can elaborate. That's all."

VI THE REST OF THE STORY

MISCELLANEOUS FILMS

Each film, no matter how many people worked on it, has what is called the "Disney Touch."
The secret is teamwork. Each character is arrived at by group effort. An artist might have
a lot of talent and come up with an excellent idea, but if, after it is thoroughly analyzed,
the character cannot be adapted and worked with by the group, we discard it.

—Walt Disney

OVER THE DECADES, Disney artists have explored such an extraordinarily diverse range of subjects and visual styles for animated films that some of their ideas defy neat categorization. While some crews considered new twists to well-known stories and varying artistic styles to present them, others sought to infuse appeal into tales that might initially seem inappropriate for animation or too offbeat to please mainstream tastes. The atmosphere at the studio encouraged them to create, investigate, and reevaluate.

Walt Disney loathed the idea of sequels. He resisted demands to reuse the enormously popular characters from *Three Little Pigs,* saying, "I've never believed in doing sequels. I don't want to waste the time I have doing a sequel; I'd rather use that time doing something new and different." But he would consider remaking a story if it could be used to experiment with a new technique, explore a new visual style, or deepen the emotional resonance of the narrative.

While the black-and-white short of Hans Christian Andersen's *The Ugly Duckling* repre-

sented one of the first attempts to generate real sympathy for a cartoon character, the more polished animation, rich color styling, and sophisticated direction of the Oscar-winning 1939 remake eclipsed the ingenuous appeal of the earlier film. *Snow White and the Seven Dwarfs, Cinderella,* and *Sleeping Beauty* all involved heroines whose gentle manners enabled them to communicate with sympathetic animals, yet each film represented a different stage in the studio artists' abilities to animate a young woman convincingly and present a story around her. A sequel wasn't always a sequel, although many of the animators feel Disney lost interest in animated features after World War II because he felt he was repeating himself to satisfy audience demand.

During the thirties, Disney often used his studio's shorts as a testing ground for ideas, techniques, and effects he planned to use in features: *The Old Mill* (1937) showcased the multiplane camera that produced a rich illusion of depth in *Snow White* and *Pinocchio.* As a result, some of the unmade films anticipate or recapitulate ideas in films that were produced.

One of the few women to achieve the rank of animator, Retta Scott visited the Southwest and did a series of sketches about a Native American boy exploring the Grand Canyon for "On the Trail." Medium: watercolor.

Jim Bodrero's comic sketches for "Sonja Heinie Fantasy" suggest a live action–animation production number, but no correspondence exists between the studio and the ice-skating movie star. Medium: gouache.

"SILLY SYMPHONIES"

During the summer of 1936, artists started developing the short "Japanese Symphony." On August 26, 1936, Bianca Majolie submitted an outline and drawings for a cartoon about a pretty moth rescued from a "dracula-like" bat by a heroic firefly amid the lanterns in a Japanese garden. (The studio would use similar insect themes in *Woodland Café*, 1937, and *The Moth and the Flame*, 1938.)

Ten months later, "Japanese Symphony" had been transformed into a "cute" romantic adventure for two Asian children, possibly set to one of the pseudo-Asian songs popular at the time—"The Japanese Sandman" or "Poor Butterfly." On June 24, 1937, Phil Horn wrote, "Wonder if you couldn't work in a little love story between a half-Americanized Japanese boy and a real Japanese girl. ("I Want To Go To Tokio" [*sic*] suggests itself as a musical theme.)"

On July 7, Grace Huntington continued the romance theme in an outline that began, "Setting: Japan in cherry blossom time. Fugi [*sic*] in the background wherever possible.... Little Japanese boy, somewhat on the order of Hiawatha as far as his actions and abilities are concerned. He is dressed

in a long Kimona [*sic*] which he trips on at the most inopportune times ... Little Japanese girl, younger than the boy, dressed in typical kimona with large obi, is a sweet, quiet, unassuming girl who loves nature ..."

A few weeks later, Majolie suggested two different story ideas. One centered on a little Japanese girl who chases a butterfly, only to let it go free when she catches it at the end of the film; the second was a fantasy about painted butterflies coming to life. A line of geishas would kneel and twirl their parasols as the camera moved in on one painted with a ring of stylized butterflies, "with wings overlapping in a kaleidoscopic effect ... and as the parasol stops revolving, they begin to animate. As they separate, their wings open like the shutter of a camera, revealing a lotus lily in the center. Lotus lily opens and reveals a beautiful butterfly asleep therein. She wakes up—yawns, stretches, and rises to a kneeling position."

The butterfly/ballerina's awakening would be followed by a musical interlude, perhaps a bubble dance in a garden fountain. When a rainstorm interrupted her dance, the ballerina would return to the shelter of the lotus; her attendants would re-

form their original circle and dissolve back into the initial design on the parasol.

The preliminary drawings for "Japanese Symphony" suggest the enchanted miniature world of the "Nutcracker" sequence in *Fantasia*. The artists used similarly structured routines involving a lovely dancer and her slightly plainer attendants twice in that film. The "Arabian Dance" depicts a long-tailed silvery white goldfish guarded by black and pink fish with shorter tails and fins; Hyacinth Hippo, the prima ballerina in "Dance of the Hours," has a clutch of hippopotamus handmaidens. The device of having the characters come to life from two-dimensional artwork occurs in the "Trepak" section of the "Nutcracker," and the artists considered reusing it in the unmade "Butterfly Ballet" segment.

While its relationship to *Fantasia* is interesting to consider, "Japanese Symphony" is probably more appealing to modern viewers as a collection of preproduction drawings than it would be as a finished film. Much of the artwork reflects the pseudo-Asian orientalism popular in the United States during the twenties and thirties. Many cartoon studios used "quaint" Asian themes in their films, as they used other racial and ethnic stereo-

types. Although acceptable at the time, these images often seem tasteless and even offensive today.

Not long after work began on "Japanese Symphony"—November 1936—a crew began developing a holiday short entitled "Santa Claus Symphony." The story centered on a little boy who shrank until he was only a few inches high and was delivered to Saint Nick's workshop along with his Christmas wish list. A request for gags from animation director Graham Heid on February 20, 1937, states, "The problem is to create situations that will allow for the development of good, cute comedy action growing out of the little kid's adventures with the toys and his meeting with Santa Claus … a human reduced to the size of a toy creates an enjoyable illusion that nearly everyone with imagination has felt at one time or another."

The Disney artists had already used Saint Nick and his toys in two "Silly Symphonies," *Santa's Workshop* (1932), and *The Night Before Christmas* (1933). They had also animated a cast of dolls in another Christmas cartoon, *Broken Toys* (1935), in which animator Grim Natwick had used the Blind Doll to test the dainty, feminine movements he would draw for Snow White.

and in the best wild style jumps over Knight.....

Bob Carr used an elegant, calligraphic drawing technique for the initial sketches for the proposed feature based on "Don Quixote." A preliminary design for Samsun Carrasco, the Bachelor of Science. Medium: India ink.

Bachelor Carrasco
Student of science

Opposite
In the most famous incident in the book, Don Quixote tilts at windmills, which he imagines are giants. The windmill sequence offered so much potential that the studio used it to test aspiring story sketch artists in late 1940s. Artist: Martin Provinson;
medium: ink, watercolor.

For "Santa Claus Symphony," the artists submitted drawings of encounters with a variety of toys and smart-aleck elves (some of whom bear a marked resemblance to the Seven Dwarfs). Inspirational artist Ferdinand Horvath sketched some charming toy characters, including a line of Dutch dolls who tap-dance in wooden shoes for a "xylophone effect." Designs for a mechanical Jewish peddler and a windup caricature of black actor Stepin Fetchit reveal the contemporary taste for ethnic humor in cartoons. The preliminary drawings have the kind of pop-eyed good humor usually seen in the cartoons Disney's old associates Hugh Harman and Rudy Ising were making at MGM during the thirties.

"Santa Claus Symphony" was being developed while *Pinocchio* was in the early stages of production, and the request for gags stresses that *"the toys should not be 'humanized'* and movement should be restricted to the action of real mechanical toys. Naturally, a reasonable amount of exaggeration can be used provided it seems plausible." Disney probably wanted to see if the animators could make appealing characters out of realistic mechanical objects—a skill they would need for Pinocchio and the figures in Geppetto's shop.

That the film was never made may indicate that Disney was satisfied with the animated toys in the tests for *Pinocchio* or that the artists had failed to come up with enough story ideas to sustain a seven-minute cartoon. Or the production may simply have fallen victim to Disney's dislike of holiday themes, which he felt restricted a film's appeal.

DOG DETECTIVES

In February 1941, Bill Cottrell and Larry Clemmons prepared storyboards for a feature based on the novel *The Hound of Florence* by Felix Salten (the author of *Bambi*). The boards show a government agent named Cummings visiting a museum and finding an ancient ring with a card that reads,

"If thou art so poor on this earth, thou must be a dog for one half of thy life; then mayest thou spend the other half as a man among men.—The Hermit of Amiata." The ring causes Cummings to change from human to canine and vice versa every night at midnight. As a dog, he's able to penetrate an espionage ring run by the villainous Dr. Cregar. Despite a number of inconvenient transformations, Cummings thwarts Cregar's schemes and rescues "counter espionage [*sic*] agent" Lulu—all in the nick of time.

Although Disney never made an animated film about a canine secret agent, *The Hound of Flo-*

rence inspired the *The Shaggy Dog* (1959), the studio's first live-action comedy. Teenager Wilby Daniels (Tommy Kirk) foils a plot to steal the plans for a secret missile after inadvertently acquiring a magic ring with similar powers. *The Shaggy Dog* scored a hit at the box office, and a sequel, *The Shaggy D.A.*, was released in 1976.

While Cottrell and Clemmons were at work on "Hound," Otto Englander and Dun Roman were developing "Inspector Bones," a spoof of the popular Sherlock Holmes films starring Basil Rathbone and Nigel Bruce. The title character was a basset hound with a fixed, deadpan expression; his round-faced assistant Dr. Beagle ("Dr. Mutton" in some of the notes) was a more loosely defined comic character with a round face and muttonchop whiskers. The preliminary watercolor drawings satirize the familiar images of the Holmes films: One shows Bones with a fez and a calabash, playing the violin next to an alley-cat-skin rug.

Although Englander and Roman considered pitting Bones and Beagle against the Moriartyesque Professor Mongrel ("The Mad Dog of London"), they abandoned the idea for "The Case of the Missing Circus." The film would open with a panning shot through a library of crime novels with punning titles ("The Thin Dog," "Fido Vance," "Mr. Mutto," etc.), and the self-conscious humor continues through the story. Bones, who lives on Barker Street, takes a case that baffles Scotty Yard. As Bones and Beagle fight their way through the cobwebby hall of Sealyham Castle, Bones remarks, "Messy business, these detective stories." The missing circus turns out to be a flea circus that Sir Cyril Sealyham, "the black sheepdog of the family," has inadvertently picked up.

"Inspector Bones" strikes the modern observer as an odd property to be considered for a feature (or even a short) at the Disney studio in 1941. The story seems superficial at best, and lacks the emotional depth and appealing characters of *Pinocchio, Dumbo,* or *Bambi.* It's closer in tone to Tex Avery's detective spoof *Who Killed Who* (1943) than to *Snow White,* but the preliminary storyboards lack the outrageous sight gags of the MGM short.

The sketches for "Inspector Bones" take on added interest because they seem to prefigure scenes in *The Great Mouse Detective* (1986). The Bones character and Basil of Baker Street assume the same pose as they examine a piece of evidence through a microscope; disguised as old salts, both characters visit seamy waterfront taverns, accompanied by their reluctant sidekicks. One sketch for "Bones" includes a canine saloon girl with a plume in her hair who

These preliminary drawings for "Don Quixote" showcase the artistic skill and visual imagination of Disney Studio artists. Artist: unknown; medium: watercolor, pastels.

resembles the mouse/chanteuse who performs "Let Me Be Good to You" in *Mouse Detective*.

John Musker and Ron Clements, two of the directors of *The Great Mouse Detective,* say they and the story crew were unaware of "Inspector Bones" when they made their film. Clements recalls screening several of the old Sherlock Holmes films, as Englander and Roman undoubtedly had forty-five years earlier; both groups of artists apparently decided to incorporate some of the same bits of business into their animated scenarios.

If "Inspector Bones" seems to foreshadow the era of renewed creativity that began in the late eighties, "Scruffy" reflects the lack of imagination that seized the studio after Walt's death. For more than two years during the late seventies, a crew headed by Ken Anderson, one of Disney's key designers, worked on this story about a Barbary ape living on the Rock of Gibraltar during World War II.

The title character recalls the determinedly happy-go-lucky animals Phil Harris voiced in *The Jungle Book* (1967), *The Aristocats* (1970), and *Robin Hood* (1973). The leader of a band of ne'er-do-well simians, Scruffy worries that Amelia, a pampered pet ape, will break up his gang, a *Lady and the Tramp* setup that had already been reused in *Aristocats*. After winning a lame conflict with an inept German spy, Scruffy and Amelia become the parents of twins. The supporting players, especially the stuffy General Gaskill and his dog, Brig, reprise the sort of "There'll always be an England" eccentrics that provided comic moments in *101 Dalmatians* but soon devolved into clichés.

Anderson's work displays its usual verve, but the threadbare premise doesn't seem to warrant the effort. That a crew could work so long and produce so many drawings for such a feeble idea is a telling comment on the state of the studio before the new generation of artists began to make their influence felt.

Drawn in a simpler style, the second version of "Don Quixote" would have been cued to Richard Strauss's tone poem. Artist: Jesse Marsh; medium: pen and ink, watercolor.

HEROINES AND ADVENTURES

Disney had considered filming *Alice in Wonderland* and a variety of fairy tales with appealing heroines during the thirties, and many unmade films center on girls or young women who embark on often improbable journies.

The sketches for a "Sonja Henie Fantasy" that Jim Bodrero drew in March and April 1946 obviously show the influence of live-action film. Rendered in watercolor, gouache, and pastels, the drawings show Henie skating with a clumsy-looking walrus and a troop of penguins in a glacial setting lit by the aurora borealis.

Whether this fantasy number would have been performed by an animated caricature of Henie or by the ice-skater herself in a live-action/animation combination is unclear. The detailed design for her costume—a spangled turquoise leotard and a spiky headdress—and the general tone of the artwork suggest the latter, as does the fact that the drawings were done while the combination feature *Song of the South* (1946) was in production. However, the Disney artists had caricatured Henie in the 1939 short *The Autograph Hound* and could easily have done so again. Either way, Bodrero's drawings could have provided the basis for a charming sequence in one of the postwar package features.

Joe Grant says that he and Dick Huemer wrote "Penelope and the 12 Months" because they liked the name. They began with a poem, then expanded it into a story for a short film about a little girl who traveled through time with the help of a magical grandfather clock. In the course of her adventures, Penelope met characters who represented the months of the year, Mother Nature and her attendant elements (rain, snow, etc.), and a leprechaun.

The preliminary art for "Penelope" includes some of the first work designer Mary Blair did for the studio. (Justly celebrated for the charm and imagination of her drawings, Blair made important contributions to *The Three Caballeros, Alice in Wonderland, Cinderella,* and other Disney features.) Grant feels that the film didn't move into the production stage because its story centered on a small child: "The audience for Disney films became more and more adult, especially after the war, so we made an effort to avoid kiddie material."

Not long after the war, Blair and other artists reworked "Penelope" into a sort of distaff version of *The Prince and the Pauper* set in Imperial Russia. The little blonde time traveler became the "small kitchen wench, Penelope," who worked for an old hag and looked just like the imperious young Queen.

At the end of December, the Queen demands a bouquet of snowdrops, declaring that "there will be no New Year's party until she has snowdrops. In fact it will go on being December … December 31, 32, 33, 34, et cetera, until she gets them." Penelope obtains the spring flowers during winter with the aid of a magic ring that is subsequently stolen by her stepmother and stepsister. The look-alike heroines would have shared a number of adventures once the question of the ring and flowers had been sorted out, including a visit to the Sultan of Turkey.

If the animators had been able to preserve the charm of Blair's preliminary sketches, either version of "Penelope" would have been a visually appealing film. However, in their book *Disney Animation: The Illusion of Life,* Frank Thomas and Ollie Johnston note:

> We all loved the crisp, fresh drawings of Mary Blair; and, since she always worked in flat colors with interesting shapes, it seemed that her work could be animated with wonderful results. Although we kept the colors, the relative shapes, and the proportions, once Mary's drawings began to move by the principles of animation that Walt had decreed they often lost the spirit of her design. It was no problem to move the drawings aristically, keeping exactly her suggestions—and some very interesting innovations came from

The semi-abstract figures in the third version of "Don Quixote" from 1951 reflect the influence of the sophisticated *New Yorker* cartoonists. Artist: unknown; medium: pen and ink, watercolor.

The vision of a couple in love galloping through the starry Western sky in "Rancho in the Sky" was probably intended for one of the post-war "package features." Artist: Dick Kelsey; medium: charcoal, pastels.

more vivid preliminary studies. Carr did finished, elaborately rendered painting; the anonymous artist employed a looser, less detailed style, using small areas of color to suggest highlights on a piece of armor or a flaring pastel line to suggest the folds of a cape. "Don Quixote" was probably derailed by the war and the studio cutbacks that followed the box-office losses of *Pinocchio* and *Fantasia*.

In 1946, a second crew, under Jesse Marsh, returned to "Don Quixote." This version would have been set to an adaptation of Richard Strauss's tone poem *Don Quixote: Fantastic Variations on a Theme of Knightly Character for Large Orchestra*, op. 35. Marsh prepared hundreds of neat pen-and-ink and watercolor cartoons, noting the musical themes that would accompany the action. He did enough rough storyboards for an entire film, beginning with a shot of the book resting on a table flanked by suits of armor, and concluding with a sort of apotheosis: After Don Quixote's death, he, Dulcinea, and Sancho Panza would ride through the clouds to a glittering castle beneath a rainbow. Like the earlier version, this incarnation of "Don Quixote" was apparently shelved before story meetings were held or dialogue prepared.

Preproduction work began for the third time in April 1951. This crew used an even simpler style that reflects the influence of such *New Yorker* cartoonists as Sol Steinberg and Otto Soglow: The rounded characters consist of little more than a few ink lines with monochromatic highlights in dull green or tan. Work on the film must have ended soon after it began, as only a few dozen drawings were completed.

In each case, the artists tried to preserve the major events of the story: Quixote's dubbing as knight by the innkeeper; his battles with the windmills and the sheep; the burning of the books of chivalry by his niece and housekeeper; the visit to the Duchess; the adventures with Cardenio and Dorotea; the encounters with the puppet theater,

these efforts—but as soon as it was necessary to tell a story with warmth and personality it all broke down.

An even more improbable set of adventures awaited the hero of another film the artists began developing around the same time: Don Quixote. Cervantes's spoof of chivalry has inspired illustrators since the publication of its first part in 1605, and Disney crews tried at least three times to adapt the picaresque classic to animation.

The initial work on the quixotic film was done around 1940 by a crew led by Bob Carr. A prolific artist, Carr did dozens of watercolors of situations and characters, many of them inspired by Velázquez and other Spanish artists. His initial studies of the Duchess, the Bachelor of Science (Samson Carrasco), et al. are as carefully detailed as the costume designs for an historical live-action film. Carr also did hundreds of drawings for preliminary storyboards, working in an elegant, calligraphic style.

Around the same time, another artist (or artists) prepared two additional sets of simpler but

the lions, and the Cart of the Parliament of Death. No one seems to have noticed just how much screen time these adventures would require, although it was not unusual for the Disney artists to storyboard more material than they needed. Veteran story man Bill Peet recalled that on *Pinocchio*, "If they had animated everything on the storyboards, it would have gone on for two days."

Another factor the artists apparently failed to consider was how to make a sympathetic character out of a lunatic. The Don Quixote the artists depicted was the farcical caricature of the novel— not the moonstruck idealist of *Man of La Mancha*. The preliminary designs stress the incongruous appearance of the Knight of the Rueful Figure, playing his scrawny physique and flaring mustache against absurdly outsized armor.

Although the drawings suggest that the contrast between reality and Quixote's fantasies could have provided some entertaining moments, none of the Disney crews tackled the challenge of condensing the rambling structure of a live-action adventure into a story that would work in animation—and could be told in less than two hours. Perhaps these daunting problems lead Disney to abandon the project despite the strength of the preliminary artwork.

AMERICANA

When the Disney artists adapted European stories, they tended to Americanize them. *Bambi* was shifted from the forests of Germany to the deciduous woods of the eastern United States; Pinocchio and Peter Pan became all-American boys. Disney was a fervent patriot ("Actually, if you could see close in my eyes, the American flag is waving in both of them, and up my spine is growing this red, white and blue stripe"), and many of his cartoons are set in an idealized late-nineteenth-century America: *Lady and the Tramp;* "Casey, the Pride of Them All" and "Johnny Fedora and Alice Blue Bon-

net" in *Make Mine Music;* "Once Upon a Wintertime" in *Melody Time;* and numerous shorts.

Although similar visions of America have appeared in countless live-action films, the Disney depictions are invariably described by critics as Walt's attempts to create an idealized fiction to replace his unhappy midwestern childhood. While there may have been a hidden wish to relive an improved version of his youth in these films, Disney may simply have realized how much a nostalgic setting appeals to American audiences.

This widely discussed Norman Rockwell Never Land provides a setting for "Barefoot Boy," an unproduced short loosely based on John Greenleaf Whittier's hoary chestnut about the supposed joys of childhood ("Outward sunshine, inward joy:/Blessings on thee, barefoot boy!"). The surviving storyboard drawings by Tom Oreb, probably done during the mid-fifties, depict the kind of "typical" boyish mischief few children of the era actually experienced. The title character smokes corn silk and gets sick, uses a frog to scare a little girl, and swipes a watermelon from a farmer's patch. (A pig eats most of it when the boy isn't looking.) The artists seem to have exhausted the poem's potential fairly quickly; a second storyboard shows apparently unrelated characters cavorting in striped gay nineties bathing suits. These boards may have been planned as parts of a single television program.

The Disney artists planned to satirize the clichés of movie Westerns in "Prairie Rhythm." Small blue pencil drawings show a novice cowboy in a series of standard adventures: He rides a bucking bronco, goes to a saloon, and falls for the singer. When he fights to defend her in a barroom brawl, she accidentally clobbers him with a chair, and the audience discovers that the action has been taking place on a movie set. "Pretty Red Wing," a short about an Indian maiden and a white trapper, also pokes fun at Hollywood Westerns. The Steinberg-esque design for the Indian chief is very reminis-

"Trees with Faces," a study of northwest coast Native American art, depicts the antics of Raven, the legendary trickster. Artist: unknown; medium: pencil, blue grease pencil.

cent of Flebus, the neurotic title character in Ernest Pintoff's 1957 cartoon.

Western themes were given a more artistic treatment in "Rancho in the Sky," an uncompleted film that may have been considered for *Make Mine Music* or one of the other package features. In a series of pretty pastel sketches, a man and a woman ride through banks of clouds that suggest canyons, mountains, etc., and gallop past the stars and the crescent moon. This dreamlike sequence was apparently set to a song: Drawings of golden stars forming a tiara illustrate a lyric in which the singer promises to gather the stars into a crown for his lover's hair.

NATIVE AMERICAN THEMES

In August 1946, Retta Scott, one of the few women to attain the rank of animator at the studio, prepared a series of dramatic watercolor and pastel sketches inspired by Southwestern Amerindian artwork for "On the Trail." (American composer Ferde Grofé's then popular *Grand Canyon Suite* includes a section called "On the Trail," and the drawings may have been intended to accompany this music.) In addition to background studies of pueblos, caverns, and eroding mesas, these striking drawings include characters based on kachina dolls, masks, and the elongated figures in sandpaintings. The story apparently involved an Indian boy and his recalcitrant burro who explore the land around their pueblo. No notes survive to indicate whether "On the Trail" would have been a feature, a short, or a section of a package feature. The revival of interest in Southwestern art during the nineties gives these drawings a contemporary look.

Amerindian art from the Pacific Northwest inspired another unfinished film, "Trees with Faces." The artwork is rendered in two styles, suggesting a live-action/animation combination, probably for an episode of the *Disneyland* television

Hiawatha and his wigwam amid the snows. The Disney artists planned two winter sequences for the film: a musical celebration of the "magic and beauty of the white forest, the ice-covered streams and falls…" and a terrible winter sent by the angry Gitche Manito (the "Great Spirit") for breaking the peace treaty. Artist: Dick Kelsey; medium: charcoal, pastels, watercolor.

Amerindian motifs have rarely been used in animation, and the preliminary drawings suggest that both "On the Trail" and "Trees with Faces" could have been visually striking films.

The Disney artists had spoofed Hollywood images of Native Americans in the "Silly Symphony" *Little Hiawatha* (1937). Walt Kelly and Grace Huntington worked on a companion cartoon, "Minnehaha," at about the same time; given Disney's dislike of sequels, it's surprising that two closely related stories were being developed simultaneously.

According to Kelly's notes, Hiawatha "is a cocky, impulsive type consistent with his established personality. Minnehaha is a naive, simple, sweet, inquisitive little girl, younger than Hiawatha, not yet aware of all life's dangers." In a series of outlines and notes prepared in October and November 1936, Kelly and Huntington considered various adventures for their child characters. Minnehaha might befriend small animals, spoiling Hiawatha's attempts to hunt them; she might fall in a river trying to rescue a doll and be saved by Hiawatha in a canoe. Hiawatha might get caught in one of his own animal traps and escape injury by falling onto a pile of blankets that Minnehaha had folded.

None of these ideas seems strong enough to sustain a film, but Kelly's drawings display their usual charm. The rather saccharine treatment of Native American children feels patronizing more than fifty years after the fact, but Hiawatha and Minnehaha fared better in these sketches than do most of the Indians—or "Injuns"—depicted in cartoons during the thirties.

HIAWATHA

Although no one seems to know what triggered Disney's interest in Henry Wadsworth Longfellow's "Hiawatha," Frank Thomas and Ollie Johnston recall that the poem held a special fascination for Walt:

show. The camera moves over a map of the Inland Passage region of Alaska as the narrator explains the ranking of the figures on a totem pole, what animals were represented, and what they symbolized. "The totem pole could be literally a family tree, a coat of arms, a monument, a tombstone, a display of wealth, or a record of tribal mythology or even a 'ridicule pole' designed to shame some person for failing to meet an obligation." The rougher charcoal sketches depict live-action footage of a Native American craftsman at work: "One of the last totem carvers is watched through the window by the children of a new generation—a generation that has forgotten his art. He is Eli Tate of the settlement of Metlakatla."

As Tate carves a miniature "good luck" totem pole, the story of Raven bringing the sun is presented in animation—indicated by a shift to more delicately rendered blue-and-black pencil drawings.

The comic antics of "Little Hiawatha,"
as drawn by Walt Kelly for
"Minnehaha," contrast sharply with
Dick Kelsey's elegant, Art Deco-
accented depiction of "the fierce
Kabibonokka," the North Wind
in Longfellow's "Hiawatha."
Medium: pencil, colored pencil,
watercolor, gouache, pastels.

Hiawatha's father, ancient Mudjekeewis, the West Wind: "On the air about him wildly/Tossed and streamed the cloudy tresses." Artist: Dick Kelsey; medium: charcoal, pastels.

He kept bringing it up over the years, trying to find the right way to do something with it. He said to us, "There's something there, y'know? Something we could do—something that's right for us. I don't know what it is or how we'd do it. Don't think of a film, don't even think of a show—don't limit your thinking to a regular theater. Maybe it's something out in the woods, or on a mountain, maybe the people are brought in—or—I don't know—but there's something there!"

Although work on the project may have begun earlier, the push to develop "Hiawatha" took place shortly after World War II. A crew of artists led by Dick Kelsey sought to trim and reorganize Longfellow's sprawling "Indian Edda" into a straightforward story that could be told in a single film.

The historic Hiawatha, an Onondaga chief who lived in what is now New York State, is credited with having organized the Iroquois Confederacy. Longfellow moved his story to the Ojibway/ Chippewa country on the southern shore of Lake Superior—the "Gitche Gummee" known to generations of students of American literature. The Disney artists preserved the transposition and researched the customs of the tribes of the northern Great Plains. They paid special attention to historic costumes, and made paper patterns for buckskin leggings and dresses. At one point, plans were made to have the characters deliver the narration in sign language, and the artists wrote to the Smithsonian Institution for information about authentic gestures.

Like the poem, the first Disney version of the story opens during a fierce intertribal war. "Gitche Manito, the mighty" (the "Great Spirit") commands them to stop fighting and announces, "I will send a Prophet to you,/A Deliverer of the nations,/Who shall guide you and shall teach you,/Who shall toil and suffer with you." The artists also kept most of Hiawatha's deeds, including his fasting and discovery of corn, his wooing of Minnehaha, and his efforts to preserve intertribal peace.

The Disney crew added a villain, Tadodaho, "the most dreaded and feared of all the warriors," who seems to have been partially based on the Pearl-Feather, the terrible magician Hiawatha defeats in part IX of the poem. Jealous of Hiawatha's prowess, Tadodaho belittles his work, murders Hiawatha's friend Chibiabos, and attempts to provoke a war with the Sioux. But the artists weakened their adaptation by omitting the requisite duel between Hiawatha and Tadodaho: The dreaded warrior dies during a blizzard just before his treachery is unmasked.

On December 8, 1948, the studio held an in-house showing of the artwork for "Hiawatha" and asked the employees to list their reactions on a questionnaire. Although everyone praised the handsome drawings, two anonymous responses cited in a report to Walt from Card Walker summarize the reservations many people expressed about the project.

Obviously leery of making another *Fantasia* that might prove too highbrow for the general public, one respondent asked, "It would make a wonderful feature, but would it be accepted? By this I mean the heaviness of the subject. Would the people going to see what they feel or expect Disney to bring them accept it? It could be an artistic triumph but would it be a success—unless considerably lightened?" While another feared that "… turning it into a 100% Disney

Hiawatha swims a river on one of his journeys. The aurora borealis appears as the ghosts of "Warriors with their plumes and war-clubs/ Flaring far away to northward." The calumet or peace-pipe of "Gitche Manito." Artist: Dick Kelsey; medium: pastels, watercolor, gouache.

cartoon takes all the adult interest from it and makes it strictly another children's picture."

Development continued on "Hiawatha" well into the next year. On August 18, 1949, Kelsey and ten other artists met to try to resolve the story problems while Disney was away. Kelsey noted:

> Walt doesn't want to make this a light thing ... he wants it [to have] a terrific musical accompaniment—almost Christ-like but not quite ... Walt said it was originally his idea to get the storyboards up to show the material we are going to work with, then call in the composer—tell the story like we just told it—let the composer write a suite called "The Hiawatha Suite"—then go back and start working from the composer's musical suite.

Animator Ollie Johnston pointed out a problem no one else seemed to have noticed—the difficulty of animating so many realistic human characters convincingly: "It looks like a hell of a job to get it on the screen unless you have Milt Kahl handle the whole job." (One of the finest draftsmen in the studio's history, Kahl was noted for his exceptional animation of human figures.)

In early September, Kelsey and Bill Cottrell prepared another treatment. This version turned the story into a flashback told to a recently arrived white missionary. The artists discarded the Tadodaho character and turned Hiawatha's battle with the Pearl-Feather into the climax of the film. Kelsey prepared additional storyboards for the new sequences, but the film seems to have been abandoned near the end of 1949, probably because of the studio's dire financial situation prior to the success of *Cinderella*.

Although he may not have known about the attempt to animate "Hiawatha," former Disney story man and comic-book artist Carl Barks subsequently sent Uncle Scrooge, Donald Duck, and Huey, Dewey, and Louie to the shores of Lake Superior in "Land of the Pigmy Indians," the main story in the June 1957 issue of the "Uncle Scrooge" comic book. The title

Feathery, semi-abstract dancers suggest that the "Surreal Short" would have lived up to its title. Artist: unknown; medium: pastels.

The snake-villain in "Hootsie the Owl" offered comic visual possibilities that intrigued the pre-production artists. Artist: unknown; medium: pencil, pastels, watercolor.

characters, the Peewee-gahs, who speak in the same meter as the poem, suggest the Puk-Wudjies, Longfellow's mischievous elves. Donald's battle with the King Sturgeon parodies Hiawatha's conquest of "the sturgeon Nahma,/Mishe-Nahma, King of Fishes." Barks's mock adventure provides a lighthearted adjunct to the beautiful but never realized film of "Hiawatha."

VISUAL EXPERIMENTS

In the years leading up to *Snow White,* Disney's unprecedented training program was focused on developing a visual style that derived from the academic tradition of fine draftsmanship and European storybook illustration. Although the look of the studio's films varied considerably over time, the animators sometimes chafed at what they perceived as the aesthetic limits of this style, especially during the postwar era, when the artists at the fledgling UPA studio led a conscious revolt against the opulent look of the Disney films.

Founded in 1943 by Stephen Bosustow, Zachary Schwartz, and David Hilberman, three former Disney artists who left the studio after the 1941 strike, UPA (United Productions of America) revolutionized the look of American cartoons by using more limited animation and flatter, contem-

porary graphics in their films. The simpler, more two-dimensional style of the UPA cartoons was influenced by the paintings of Picasso, Matisse, Modigliani, Klee, and other modern artists as well as the work of Sol Steinberg and the sophisticated cartoonists at the *New Yorker.* This aesthetic shift is clearly visible in UPA's "Mr. Magoo" series and the Oscar-winning short *Gerald McBoing-Boing.*

Although neither style is inherently superior, the UPA films received widespread praise not only in the popular press but also in art magazines that had previously ignored the existence of animation. Almost invariably, the authors of these articles contrasted what they saw as the innovations of UPA with the "old-fashioned" Disney style. In response, the artists at the Disney studio began to experiment with flatter graphics in some shorts, notably, the Oscar-winning *Toot, Whistle, Plunk, and Boom* (1953). But many of the earliest and boldest stylistic innovations were restricted to films that remained uncompleted.

The desire to reflect the look of modern fine art is particularly evident in the preliminary sketches for "One More Spring" by Tom Oreb and Jesse Marsh. The angular, somewhat distorted figures are modeled after the work of Picasso (and, in a few places, Rousseau and Dalí), including a nude painted by a slovenly artist.

As no story notes or synopses survive, it's impossible to decipher the plot of the film, which seems to revolve around a serenely grubby Parisian artist and a look-alike American businessman. Nor is it clear how these characters relate to the epigraph from *Measure for Measure* that would appear on the screen after the titles: "But man, proud man,/Dressed in a little brief authority,/Whose glassy essence, like an angry ape's,/Cuts such capers before high heaven/As make the angels weep."

The influence of *Gerald McBoing-Boing, Willie the Kid,* and other UPA shorts involving children can be seen even more clearly in the story

sketches and rhyming narration for the unmade "Rudy Doodle." The title character is a simple outline figure of a boy in a cap and saddle shoes who makes even simpler drawings on an easel: "To be a Rembrandt or Titian/Isn't Rudy's fond ambition/ For Doodling's his fav'rite game." Rudy's sketches enable him to visit "Doodleland," where he can affect what goes on around him by drawing new props, doorways, etc., a device used in the television series *Winky Dink and You* (1953–57). "Rudy Doodle" may have been intended as a theatrical short or as a cartoon for TV.

Grant recalls beginning work on "Lorenzo the Magnificent" during World War II. The story centers on a large Persian cat whose tail comes to life, causing numerous complications. The drawings of Lorenzo parallel the style Steinberg was developing around the same time, and anticipate the look of Ronald Searle's early work: The title character consists of little more than a cat-shaped outline with a simplified face and two points for ears.

The Disney artists ventured even further from their traditional look and subject matter in the postwar "Surrealist Short." The pastel sketches show a heart splitting in two and the halves form-

ing feathery-looking dancers. They're accompanied by jazz musicians who seem to be department store window dummies, and a chorus line of disembodied gloves, hats, and stockings that may also be part of a shop display. (The drawings are oddly reminiscent of Ub Iwerks's *Merry Mannequins* (1937), a cartoon about two store window dummies who perform what is essentially an animated version of a Fred Astaire–Ginger Rogers number.) The jazz musicians and dancing figures suggest that the film may have been planned for *Make Mine Music* or another package feature.

An effortless surrealism pervades Albert Hurter's idea sketches for "Hootsie the Owl," a film the artists worked on at various times over three decades. The title character is a misfit, an owl who was born during the day and prefers to sleep at night. His unconventional schedule embarrasses his parents and leaves him without friends, enabling a conniving snake to trick him into stealing the eggs of the other owls. But when he learns that the snake plans to eat the eggs, Hootsie rescues them just before they hatch. The excitement of restoring the newborn owlets to their parents exhausts Hootsie and enables him to return to a proper regimen of

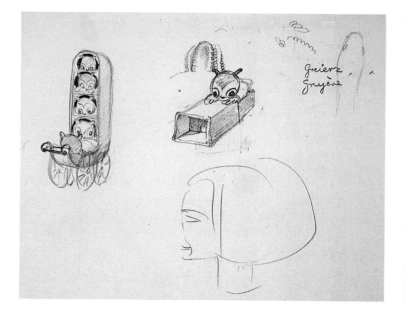

sleeping all day and staying up all night.

Development on the film apparently began during the war, but the project was repeatedly suspended and revived: Ron Hall worked on it as late as 1969. Hootsie doesn't seem to have interested the artists as much as the snake, who looks more like a comic sidekick than a villain. (Sketches from 1969 give him hypnotic powers reminiscent of Kaa's in *The Jungle Book*, 1967.) Some of the drawings have a zany simplicity that brings to mind the Jay Ward menagerie, but the most amusing artwork is Hurter's.

Story man Ted Sears noted, "Each time a new subject was planned, Albert was consulted and given free reign to let his imagination wander, creating strange animals, plants, scenery, or costumes that might serve as models for the forthcoming production." When Hurter drew the snake, he gave the character a top hat, an opera cape, and a glove on his tail that functioned as a hand; he covered pages with sketches of mother owls pushing elongated prams full of eggs, owl villages straddling tree limbs, and proper-looking owls going about their daily business. His charmingly skewed vision of life in a logical yet absurd city of owls gives "Hootsie" an appeal the story otherwise lacks.

"DESTINO"

The most fantastic of the uncompleted Disney films was "Destino" (1946), a collaboration between Walt Disney and Salvador Dalí. It's difficult to conceive of two less compatible-sounding artists. How could any project possibly reconcile Dalí's flamboyant eccentricity with Disney's wholesome vision of Americana?

The origins of the project are unclear. Dalí was working in Hollywood at the time on Alfred Hitchcock's *Spellbound* (1945) and other films. Disney, who was always eager to keep up with his live-action counterparts, may have approached him. The ingenuous fantasy of such prewar shorts as *Gulliver Mickey* (1934) and *Thru the Mirror* (1936) may have appealed to Dalí and led him to initiate the project. Many contemporary observers considered the collaboration improbable, and skeptical articles appeared in the popular press: "Disney and Dali Join for Weird Film Opus"; "Masters of Mickey Mouse and Limp Watch Team Up." In an interview printed in the *Los Angeles Times*, Disney complained, "The thing I resent most is people who try to keep me in well-worn grooves. We have to keep breaking new trails. We were panned for *Fantasia*, yet its audience keeps building each year."

"Destino" would have been set to Armando Dominguez's ballad about a young woman's search for her destined true love; Disney had acquired the rights to the song sometime earlier, probably in conjunction with the Latin American films. John Hench, who worked with Dalí on the storyboards, feels that the title had more appeal for the artist than the music. ("He had a thing for destiny.")

"Destino" was conceived of as a live-action/animation sequence for one of the package films. As a young man and woman fought external obstacles to realize their love, the action would shift from dance to animation and vice versa. At one point, Russian-born ballet star André Eglevsky was considered for the male role.

None of the two storyboards and five written treatments that were prepared for the film describes a conventional narrative. Some versions show the balletic pas de deux mutating into a semblance of a baseball game. In an interview with Bob Thomas, Dalí declared, "Baseball, it is fascinating. About the game, I know nothing. But as an artist, I am obsessed." Other versions open with an actor (a workman or the male dancer) watching Dalí at an easel and asking the meaning of the imagery in the painting (which would include one of his famous limp watches), to which the artist would reply:

> What you see here are just symbols. Surrealism is like a new language. Every object means something other than what it naturally appears to be. This watch for instance—it symbolizes the relativity of time. Depending on the circumstances, in love for instance, one minute of waiting may seem like a thousand years … Or an hour may pass as quickly as if it were a few seconds. The time of human beings is different than mechanical time. It's flexible and viscous, like the time in dreams.

The surviving storyboards include evocative elements that recur in Dalí's paintings: bleak, rocky landscapes that stretch into infinity; grotesquely elongated figures supported on wire crutches; brooding, ruined buildings; mechanical devices (in this case, telephones) that sprout the spindly limbs of daddy longlegs spiders; and the infamous melted watches.

At one point, the girl is pursued up a cliff by a horde of figures with eyeballs for heads: They represent the eyes of public opinion trying to thwart her efforts to attain happiness. (In one version, they flare like giant flashbulbs.) Newspapers with scorpion legs join the pursuit until the girl takes refuge inside a giant whelk shell. When the shell falls off the precipice, the camera pulls back to reveal the cliff's resemblance to a truncated torso.

Some of the most striking effects showcase Dalí's ability to create double images through the interplay of positive and negative space. A group of elements seen through the mouth of a ruined tunnel forms the head of Chronos, the god of time. In another sequence, the shadow of a bell in a campanile becomes the skirt of a ballet dancer.

In a 1989 interview, Hench described the way in which he and Dalí worked during their collaboration:

> Dalí would usually do a key position and then I'd fill in the in-betweens, trying to segue from one area to another. He had a concept that he was going to stick to in a broad sense, but he shared a lot with Walt in his inventive ability. Walt always came in with a lot more situations than perhaps a story could hold, and Dalí was a great deal the same way. Every morning he had new ideas. I'm sure we could never have fitted all of them in the original time allotted.

Disney later seconded this evaluation: "Ordinarily good story ideas don't come easily and have to be fought for, but with Dalí, it was exactly the reverse. He constantly bubbled with new ideas, not only for the picture, but in fact, they spilled over into all directions, such as machines, furniture, jewelry …"

The artists prepared a single test for the film, in which two distorted heads mounted on tortoise shells glide toward each other. The negative space between them becomes the figure of the ballerina/ heroine (with a baseball for a head). Shortly after the seventeen-second test was completed, "Destino" was abandoned for unknown reasons. Hench believes that Disney foresaw the end of the package features, although he went on to release *Fun and Fancy Free* in 1947 and *Melody Time* in 1948. Disney later said, "It was certainly no fault of Dalí's that the project we were working on was not completed—it was simply a case of policy changes in our distribution plans."

Despite the failure of "Destino," the principals remained on good terms. Disney described Dalí as "a friend, a very swell guy, and a person whom I thoroughly enjoyed working with." On a subsequent visit to Hollywood, Dalí rode the miniature train that circled Disney's house in Holmby Hills, but "he was so impressed by the completeness of the detail, he felt it would be dangerous because such perfection of detail would inevitably provoke accidents such as real trains have … or even sabotage … like miniature train wreckers!" Disney visited Dalí's home in Spain during the fifties and reportedly proposed that they collaborate on "The Adventures of Don Quixote" or "El Cid."

Not long after "Destino" was shelved, many of the drawings for it were stolen. Some of them were purchased by an art dealer in New York and eventually returned to the studio. Others, including the artwork for the seventeen-second test, have never been found. It was an unhappy coda to a singular but apparently felicitous meeting of minds.

DISNEY REDUX

I think the most interesting thing about animation is that every bloody frame of it starts out as a totally blank piece of paper—on which you can find anything you can think of.

— Roy E. Disney

D URING THE MID-EIGHTIES, the Disney animators began to emerge from the lethargy that had gripped the studio since Walt's death. By the end of the decade, their features had eclipsed the work of the rival Don Bluth and Amblimation studios, and Disney once again dominated the field as absolutely as it had during the thirties.

The renaissance of the animation department was the result of major changes at the parent Walt Disney Company. The Disney family's management of the company ended in June 1984 when Ron Miller, Walt's son-in-law, resigned under fire after fending off a takeover bid from financier Saul P. Steinberg. Former Paramount president Michael Eisner became chairman of the board and CEO; Warner Bros. vice president Frank Wells, president and COO; Jeffrey Katzenberg, a longtime associate of Eisner's, became studio chairman. One of the key players in this change was Roy Edward Disney (the son of Walt's older brother, Roy Oliver, who managed the studio's finances):

When that board meeting was over and Michael and Frank had been elected to the company, Michael looked at me and said, "Now that all this is over, what do you want?" After about fifteen seconds of thought, I said, "Why don't you give me animation?" Of all the bits and pieces of this place, animation was probably—from the point of view of outsiders coming in, particularly people who are used to conceiving and shooting and releasing a film over a nine-month span—the hardest thing to understand and the one that would take the most time to find a rhythm of dealing with.

"I figured, well, I grew up around it, I must know something about it—by osmosis, if nothing else--," Disney continues with a chuckle. "I was appalled to learn how little I really knew about the process; I think all of us were appalled to learn how little we really knew about it."

The new management team was faced with the immediate task of completing *The Black Cauldron,* which was overdue and overbudget. Preproduction had also begun on the next feature project, *The Great Mouse Detective,* but work on it had been suspended during the corporate siege.

"John [Musker] and Ron [Clements], God bless them, had that whole story up on boards," explains Disney. "They showed me a bunch of the material, and I said, 'This is cute, this is really sort

The title character from "Hootsie the Owl" finally looks tired enough to sleep through the day, as a proper owl should. Artist: Jack Miller; medium: pastels, watercolor.

Opposite
The Swan of Tuonela guides the boat carrying the Viking chieftain through caverns and past treacherous whirlpools. Artists: Sylvia Holland, Joe Stahley; medium: pastels.

of nice.' So I dragged Michael and Frank down within a couple of weeks of their having come into the company—this was before Jeffrey even got there. Ron and John had storyboards lined up down the halls and through doorways: There must have been forty boards. Neither Michael nor Frank had a clue what they were looking at; they were standing in that narrow hall, trying to see the drawings. Michael saw enough of it to say, 'That is cute, we probably should go ahead with it.' I've always thought that if there was ever a turning point in the recent history of the studio, that was the moment. It didn't seem so at the time of course, because they never do, but that film served as a training ground for the executives, as well as the animation crew."

Looking back over the period that followed his uncle's death, Disney comments, "The animation department was sort of allowed to do what it would for a number of years. You accepted whatever came out and tried to sell it. We tried to make some cuts and work with *Cauldron,* but there was only so much we could do, because it was so near completion at that point."

All the members of the new team believed that animation was "the heart and soul" of both the studio and the company. They stepped up the recruiting campaign for young artists and accelerated the studio's somewhat belated entry into the field of computer animation. As senior vice president and, later, president of feature animation, Peter Schneider was put in charge of the department. Schneider, who had helped to organize the Los Angeles Olympic Arts Festival, had a background in theater rather than animation. He recalls his initiation into the process:

When I arrived here, I walked into a room with John Musker, Ron Clements, Burny Mattinson, Dave Mitchner, George Scribner, Rick Rich, and about fifteen other people. They all crossed their hands and asked, "What are you doing here, and

A stagecoach takes author Hans Christian Andersen from Copenhagen to his native village of Odense. Artist: unknown; medium: watercolor.

A preliminary drawing of Samsun Carrasco, the Bachelor of Science for the "Don Quixote" feature. Artist: Bob Carr; medium: watercolor, India ink.

what are you going to do for us?" I gave the same answer I'd give today: "I'm here to help you create the movies you want to make and to help you get the decisions, the money, and the talent you need to make those movies."

They didn't get it, so I asked, "What problems are you having?" Dave Mitchner said they couldn't get a decision as to whether to get Melissa Manchester to sing this song or to get somebody else—and they'd been waiting for this decision for three months. I called Jeffrey and we agreed that we would go ahead with Melissa. Next! I suppose they were blown away that I was able to get a decision made within thirty seconds, but my job is to help them get decisions made so they can make their movies within the structure of the company.

The Black Cauldron (1985) failed to generate much excitement. But The Great Mouse Detective (1986) became the first in a string of hits that broke box-office records and re-established the Disney studio's position at the forefront of both animation and family entertainment: Who Framed Roger Rabbit (1988), Oliver & Company (1988), The Little Mermaid (1989), The Rescuers Down Under (1990), Beauty and the Beast (1991), Aladdin (1992), and The Lion King (1994). Roger Rabbit garnered four Academy Awards, including a special one for animation director Richard Williams; Mermaid, Beauty, Aladdin, and The Lion King received Oscars for Best Song and Best Original Score. Beauty and the Beast became the first animated feature to receive an Academy Award nomination for Best Picture.

In 1992, seven people from Disney Feature Animation and three from the computer animation studio PIXAR shared an additional Academy Award for scientific and technical achievement for the development of CAPS (Computer Animation Production System). This sophisticated combination of

In this sketch for "Sonja Heinie Fantasy," the ice skater skips lightly from floe to floe; the penguins accompanying her prove less graceful. Artist: Jim Brodrero; medium: gouache.

hardware and software allowed the artists to re-create visual effects that had become too expensive to do by hand and introduced new approaches to traditional animation in a variety of areas, from ink and paint to scene planning and cinematography. Recalls Disney,

> Dave English came to me and said, "You know, they're doing a lot of really interesting things with computers these days, and you ought to take a look." It was just so obvious when you started looking around that this could be a tool for an artist that would change things—in much the way that the multiplane camera or the Xerox process did. I sold it to Frank Wells by saying we're going to replace the ink and paint department if you'll give us $15 or $16 million. I had a date with all the PIXAR guys when they were down

to get the first check, which was for $5 million. They were all in Frank's office, so I just sort of wandered into the room and stood at the back, looking over the scene. Frank looked up at me and said, "What are you doing here?" And I said, "I'm just here to make sure you sign that check!"

"The computer has opened up such a world of possibilities for us in terms of what a film can look like," Disney adds. "It gives you avenues into more kinds of stories: You just keep saying, There's more we can do, there's more we can do."

A NEW APPROACH

The animated films made by the new Disney team—and the features that remain in development or have

"Prelude to War": Hands raise a sword bearing the Rising Sun of the Japanese flag. Artist: Martin Provinson; medium: charcoal.

been shelved—were created through a new system that combines elements of the visually oriented development process of the thirties and the use of scripts that began shortly before Walt's death.

"Walt Disney had his process for making these movies that was also very reflective of his skills as a storyteller and as a filmmaker," says Katzenberg thoughtfully. "I couldn't sit down and tell the story of *The Lion King*, scene by scene and character by character, which is what Walt did. He could conjure these things up in his mind, inspired by a classic piece of literature or, in later years, contemporary literature. I don't have that skill, but I brought a discipline that I understood that begins with developing a screenplay. We've learned that the screenplay is an important stepping-stone to the story, but it's not like a live-action movie, where something goes directly from the page to the screen. There are so many in-between steps in which the translation is not as predictable. We develop the characters, production design, layout, background, palette, as the screenplay is being written."

In response to an increasing demand for films, and the accelerated pace of production, the new

Dramatic images from the forties: The Valkyries leave their rock to snatch up souls of dying heroes in "The Ride of the Valkyries." Artist: Kay Neilsen; medium: charcoal, pastels.

197

An image from the "Insect Ballet" planned for
Fantasia: a pastel drawing of cobra lilies emulates
the look of lacquer-work. Artist: Ethel Kulsar.

Opposite
An insect orchestra for "Chanticleer." Artist:
unknown; medium: watercolor.

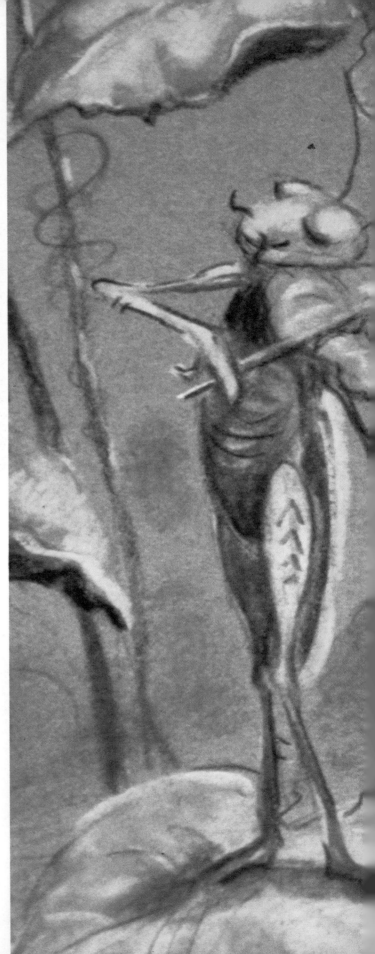

management devised a process that emphasizes team effort and the division of labor rather than relying on the taste of a single individual.

"I think when Walt was alive, he was everything: producer, storyteller, director—the whole shebang rolled into one," says Schneider. "When you lose a figure like Walt, the first tendency, which they tried for twenty years, is to replace him with one man. I'm not sure you can replace one person with one person. I think we have to look at animation more structurally: As you do in live-action filmmaking, you have a producer, a director, a screenwriter, a designer, who make a production team. Together they form a very strong foundation for making a movie.

"The concept of building a pyramidal structure and putting people in charge of specific areas is extremely important," he adds. "The reason we've had such rich looks in art direction is because we had an art director—chosen by the director—who changed with each picture.

Each editor brings a different way of telling a story with pictures. As you add more creative points of view from artists who are skilled in various areas, the pictures get better."

One of the primary sources of ideas for the films is the executive pitch, a method that is often used in live-action studios. Thomas Schumacher, senior vice president of feature animation who supervises the story development, explains, "Within the development department, there are creative executives, just like any studio. But the normal studio creative executive is out cultivating pitches, trying to get writers to come in and pitch ideas. We don't really do that. For the most part, our executives are out looking for writers who will write on assignment because although we accept outside story pitches, our ideas are generally developed internally by our staff and artists."

A problem that Walt Disney articulated decades earlier continues to vex writers whose experience is restricted to live action: Animation and live-action filmmaking are distinct media with unique strengths and weaknesses. Effects that work in a live-action film may not work in an animated one and vice versa.

"One should only do things in animation that require animation and that are animatable," states Schneider. "In *Beauty and the Beast*, Beast and the enchanted objects could only be realized in animation; in *Aladdin*, it was the Genie; in *Pocahontas*, it's the magic of the world; in *The Hunchback of Notre Dame*, it's the Hunchback and the gargoyles and another special vision of the world."

Many of the ideas for films are suggested by the members of the animation staff at meetings called "Gong Shows," after the Chuck Barris TV program. Twice a year at Disney's Glendale facility and once each year at the Florida studio, notices circulate announcing an upcoming session. Any full-time employee of the feature animation department—animators, cleanup artists, secretaries, production assistants—can give a brief presentation of an idea before an audience that includes most of the studio's senior personnel, including Thomas Schumacher, Peter Schneider, Roy Disney, and, usually, Michael Eisner. {Katzenberg also attended during his tenure at the studio.} The presenters accompany their pitches with visuals that range from rough sketches to elaborate paintings and, in one case, plastic toys. (Directors may present ideas at these sessions, or to the executives directly.)

Two versions of "Penelope": Joe Grant and Dick Huemer originally envisioned a story in which a little girl would travel through a magic grandfather clock to meet various symbolic characters, including a leprechaun and the months of the year. A later version of the story turned Penelope into an Imperial Russian princess. Artist: Mary Blair; medium: watercolor.

Opposite
Chanticleer visits one of the less edifying denizens of the farmyard he supervises. Artist: Marc Davis; medium: watercolor, pen and ink.

This caricature of Louis Armstrong as a frog was designed for a sequence in "Musicana" set in a Southern bayou . Artist: Ken Anderson; medium: watercolor, pen and ink.

"What we do here is unique in the annals of moviemaking, and the kind of stories we look for are usually not what people in the entertainment industry are developing," explains Schneider. "We've discovered that the best way to find ideas is to ask the artists who make the movies, who understand what animation is all about. So most of our stories come from the artists themselves: *The Little Mermaid, Pocahontas,* and *Hercules* are all Gong Show ideas."

Despite the name, there is no gong in the room, and it's unusual for a presentation to be cut off. The atmosphere at the "Gong Shows" varies from session to session, although one animator characterized them as "very relaxed and very nervous—the executives are relaxed and the presenters are nervous." All the artists who have attended shows agree that the senior executives are "very gracious about giving their full attention to every idea—no matter how outrageous or terrible." The thirty or more presenters all hope to have the elusive idea "that's going to hit them right at that moment. Some stories that seem like obvious choices once they're in production may be hard to recognize at a presentation."

In addition, the studio will occasionally enter into an agreement to make a film proposed by another production entity, such as the stop-motion features directed by Henry Selick, *Tim Burton's Nightmare Before Christmas, James and the Giant Peach,* and *Toy Story,* the first computer animation feature being directed by John Lasseter at PIXAR. (Burton, Selick, and Lasseter are all former Disney artists.)

Once an idea is "green-lighted," it enters development, a process that varies in its details from project to project, depending on the nature of the story, the format of the original material, and the availability of artists.

"We have to identify what the movie is about before we deal with the story—the thematic values that form the underpinning of the movie, on which you hang the story," says Schneider. "An easy example is *Beauty and the Beast,* which is 'Don't judge a book by its cover.' Once you have that thematic underpinning, the story needs to support the concept.

"The most important things for us are the outline and treatment of the story to give us a beginning, a middle, and an end," he adds. "Once we have those, we start both visual storytelling and written storytelling. You can't just develop it visually, and you can't just develop the words on the page. It's a blend of these two ideas that ultimately leads you to success."

The visual and verbal development Schneider describes may require two or more years. Directors and animators have to be assigned; voices cast and recorded; dialogue written and rewritten; lyricists and composers found. Key artists do extensive research that may involve travel to other continents. Designs have to be worked out and approved for the characters, backgrounds, effects, and computer-generated elements.

As in the past, everything has to be translated into storyboards. Writing and boarding usually go on simultaneously as the story crew refines the characters, delineates their relationships, and invents business for them. At every step, the work is discussed, analyzed, criticized, and reworked in a seemingly endless succession of meetings that recalls the ones Disney held with his artists sixty years earlier.

The material is continually revised, even after the animation has begun, as early scenes may redefine characters or suggest new story possibilities. Chip, the pert teacup in *Beauty and the Beast,* began as a very minor character, but the combination of the vocal and animated performances proved so winning, the role was expanded.

"The pleasure and the frustration of making these movies is that the process allows you to think about every moment, and redo every line and every sketch five times," continues Schneider wryly.

The elegant lion and his rhinoceros attendant for a scene illustrating African folk music. Artist: Ken Anderson; medium: watercolor, pen and ink

"Because the process is invisible financially when you do these things, you think it's so easy and cost efficient to do it—when in reality it's tremendously expensive and the impact is enormous."

As Schneider suggests, the stakes are high. Although Disney executives refuse to discuss the budgets of their

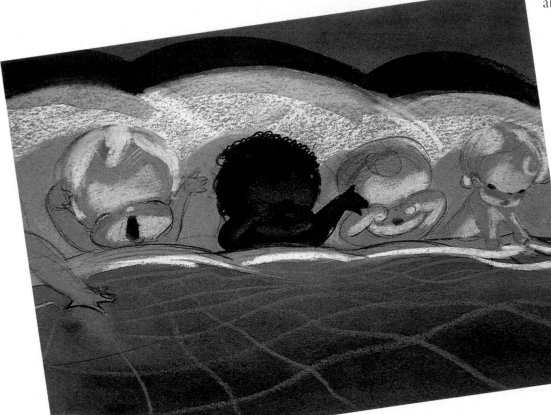

films, entertainment industry estimates place the cost of the animated features in the $25 to $35 million range—considerably less than a big-budget live-action feature. But a hit film on the order of *Beauty and the Beast, Aladdin,* or *The Lion King* can earn hundreds of millions of dollars at domestic and foreign box offices in addition to substantial revenues from videocassette sales, merchandise, licensing, and theme park attractions.

Under the new management, The Walt Disney Company has grown into a $10 billion business, with motion pictures accounting for about

$4 billion of that sum. In 1994, the company was shaken by the death of Frank Wells in a helicopter accident in April, followed by the highly publicized resignation of Jeffrey Katzenberg in August. Despite the loss of these key players, production and preproduction work continues on a full slate of films. Schneider believes that the studio has been able to continue because its work is artist-driven:

The success of this department is analogous to the successes in the live-action business during the seventies, when you had kids coming out of film school—George Lucas, Steven Spielberg, John Landis, Robert Zemeckis—who believed passionately that they had something important to say that had never been said, and that they could say it better than their predecessors and mentors. Between '75 and '83, a group of kids came out of film and art school who said, "This is a medium where I can make a difference and say something and be as good or even better than the old Disney artists." Whether or not they are is immaterial; it's the belief in themselves that they can do better that's significant. These artists passionately believe that they have something to say that's important to say in this medium and that they can do it better than their predecessors. During the past decade, they've matured to the point where they can realize their visions. It's been exciting to watch them come of age, and we here at Disney have given them the resources to do it.

During the thirties, Walt Disney publicly dismissed the idea that his studio's output could be called art—a denial many observers disputed. In addition to its obvious ties to traditional fine draftsmanship and the graphic arts, the animated feature has curious affinities with opera. Each represents a synergetic fusion of movement, acting, choreography, music, writing, design, and color that requires a large crew of diverse artists to achieve. Largely pioneered at the Disney studio, character animation, the art of making a drawn figure move with a style that delineates his or her personality,

Cutesy infants fall asleep and are borne by storks to unsuspecting parents in the "Baby Ballet" for *Fantasia*. Artist: Mary Blair; medium: pastels.

ranks with jazz and musical comedy as a uniquely American contribution to the fine arts.

The preponderance of inferior Saturday morning cartoon shows during the sixties and seventies caused many Americans to dismiss the medium as a mindless children's entertainment. During the eighties, the first features from Amblimation, Don Bluth, and the new Disney artists infused new life into the animated feature. These successes were followed by a boom in more sophisticated prime-time cartoon shows, led by *The Simpsons* (1989) on the Fox Network. During the nineties, the studio's young animators have once again proved what Walt Disney and his staff established decades earlier: A good animated film will appeal equally to the least sophisticated and the most sophisticated members of the audience.

"I think our role at the senior management level is to create the environment that enables the artists to do what they do best," concludes Schneider. "Secondarily, to guide them in the area of story, and that is ultimately where these movies have been most successful: storytelling. These artists keep pushing the frontiers of animation one step further every time out, which is really their desire and their vision—we're just enabling them to do it. We give them the money, we give them the tools, and we give them encouragement."

The extraordinary success of the recent Disney films has not only ensured the survival of the studio's animation department but has also stimulated a record level of feature production in America. Still, whenever a new feature appears, it is inevitably measured against the standard of excellence Walt Disney set during the thirties and forties. In response to the inevitable questions about the shadow of his uncle that looms over the studio he founded and the entire animation industry, Roy Disney replies:

> What I've always said about Walt is not that he's looking over our shoulder but that he's just ahead of us. The quality of the past films makes you want to live up to them and work at that level all the time. I remember at one of the early screenings of *Beauty and the Beast* in Hollywood, I walked out with Frank [Thomas] and Ollie [Johnston]. I was thinking, "This is really a hell of a movie," and I said something to the effect of, "Well, what do you think?" They said, "Well, it's pretty good—it's almost as good as we used to do." It's important that they feel that way, and it's important that the standard they set is still there, because it will always remain the damned carrot in front of the donkey.

*What I see way off there is too nebulous to describe, but it looks
big and glittering. That's what I love about this business, the certainty
that there is always something bigger and more exciting just around
the bend; and the uncertainty of everything else.*

—Walt Disney on the future of animation, 1940

Disney artist Tom Sito pokes fun at the author's research by suggesting Walt Disney came up with the idea for *He-Man and the Masters of the Universe* forty-odd years before the fact.

BIBLIOGRAPHY

BOOKS

Andersen, Hans Christian. *Eighty Fairy Tales*. New York: Pantheon, 1982.—. *The Steadfast Tin Soldier*. Retold by Simon Lewin. New York: Disney Press, 1991.

The Carl Barks Library of Walt Disney's Donald Duck 1942–1949. Scottsdale, AZ: Another Rainbow, 1984.

Barks, Carl. *Uncle Scrooge McDuck: His Life and Times*. Berkeley: Celestial Arts, 1987.

Bettelheim, Bruno. *The Uses of Enchantment: The Meaning and Importance of Fairy Tales*. New York: Vintage, 1977.

Cervantes, Miguel de. *Don Quixote*. New York: New American Library, 1964.

Cowles, Fleur. *The Case of Salvador Dalí*. Boston: Little, Brown, 1959.

Dahl, Roald. *The Gremlins from the Walt Disney Production*. New York: Random House, 1943.

Disney, Walt, and H. Marion Palmer. *Donald Duck Sees South America*. New York: D. C. Heath, 1945.

Dorfman, Ariel, and Armand Mattelart. *How to Read Donald Duck: Imperialist Ideology in the Disney Comic*. Translated by David Kunzle. New York: International General, 1975.

Grant, John. *Encyclopedia of Walt Disney's Animated Characters*. New York: Hyperion, 1993.

Hollis, Richard, and Brian Sibley. *Walt Disney's Snow White and the Seven Dwarfs: The Making of the Classic Film*. New York: Hyperion, 1994.

Horn, Maurice, ed. *The World Encyclopedia of Comics*. New York: Avon, 1977.

Johnston, Ollie, and Frank Thomas. *Walt Disney's Bambi: The Story and the Film*. New York: Stewart, Tabori and Chang. 1990.

Longfellow, Henry Wadsworth. *The Song of Hiawatha*. New York: Bounty Books, 1968.

Maltin, Leonard. *Of Mice and Magic: A History of American Animated Cartoons*. New York: McGraw-Hill, 1980.

—. *The Disney Films*. New York: Crown, 1984.

Osborne, Chase S., and Stellanova Osborne. *Hiawatha with Its Original Indian Legends*. Lancaster, PA: The Jacques Cattell Press, 1944.

Palmer, H. Marion. *Walt Disney's Surprise Package*. New York: Simon & Schuster, 1944.

Peary, Gerald, and Danny Peary, eds. *The American Animated Cartoon: A Critical Anthology*. New York: Dutton, 1980.

Peet, Bill. *Bill Peet: An Autobiography*. Boston: Houghton Mifflin, 1989.

Rawls, Walton. *The Best of Disney Military Insignia from World War II*. New York: Abbeville, 1992.

Schickel, Richard. *The Disney Version*. New York: Simon & Schuster, 1968.

Shale, Richard. *Donald Duck Joins Up: The Walt Disney Studio During World War II*. Ann Arbor: UMI Press, 1982.

Solomon, Charles. *Enchanted Drawings: The History of Animation*. New York: Alfred A. Knopf, 1989.

Thomas, Bob. *Walt Disney: An American Original*. New York: Simon & Schuster, 1976.

Thomas, Frank, and Ollie Johnston. *Disney Animation: The Illusion of Life*. New York: Abbeville, 1981.

———. *Too Funny for Words: Disney's Greatest Sight Gags*. New York: Abbeville, 1987.

Treglown, Jeremy. *Roald Dahl: A Biography*. New York: Farrar, Strauss, Giroux, 1994.

ARTICLES

Canemaker, John. "The *Fantasia* That Never Was." *Print*, January/February, 1988.

Cawley, John. "Walt Disney and 'The Gremlins,' an Unfinished Story." *American Classic Screen*, IV, Spring 1980.

Dahl, Roald. "Here They Are!" *Cosmopolitan*, December 1942.

Miller, Arthur. "Masters of Mickey Mouse and Limp Watch Team Up." *Los Angeles Times*, April 7, 1946.

Salkin, Leo. "Working for Walter Lantz in the '30s." *The Art of the Animated Image: An Anthology*, Charles Solomon, ed. Los Angeles, American Film Institute, 1987.

Solomon, Charles. *"It Wasn't Always Magic." Los Angeles Times*, October 7, 1990, calendar section.

———. "M-O-U-S-E: The World's Most Famous Rodent Nears 60, and He's Had More Lives Than a Cat." *Los Angeles Times*, November 13, 1988, calendar section (Orange County edition).

———. "'We're Still the Artists' Studio:' An Interview with Peter Schneider." *Animation Magazine*, Spring 1989.

———. "'Why Don't You Give Me Animation?' An Interview with Roy Disney." *Animation Magazine*, Spring 1989.

Thomas, Bob. "Disney and Dalí Join for Weird Film Opus," *Cincinnati Times Star*, April 10, 1946.

Wallace, Irving. "Mickey Mouse, and How He Grew." *Collier's*, April 9, 1949.

Young, Jordan R. "Disney and Dalí's 'Destino': A Tale of Two Visionaries. *Los Angeles Times*, calendar section, January 29, 1989.

SPECIAL PUBLICATIONS

Adamson, Joe. "From This You Are Making a Living?" Oral history interviews with Dick Huemer, Los Angeles: American Film Institute, 1968–69.

Justice, Bill. *Justice for Disney*. Dayton, OH: Tomart Publications, 1992.

Solomon, Charles, ed. *The Art of the Animated Image: An Anthology*. Los Angeles: The American Film Institute, 1987.

INDEX

Page numbers in *italics* refer to captions.